U. S. Grant

The American Crisis Series
Books on the Civil War Era
Steven E. Woodworth, Associate Professor of History,
Texas Christian University
SERIES EDITOR

U. S. Grant
The Making of a General, 1861–1863

Michael B. Ballard

ROWMAN & LITTLEFIELD PUBLISHERS, INC.
Lanham • Boulder • New York • Toronto • Oxford

ROWMAN & LITTLEFIELD PUBLISHERS, INC.

Published in the United States of America
by Rowman & Littlefield Publishers, Inc.
A wholly owned subsidary of
The Rowman & Littlefield Publishing Group, Inc.
4501 Forbes Boulevard, Suite 200, Lanham, Maryland 20706
www.rowmanlittlefield.com

PO Box 317
Oxford
OX2 9RU, UK

Distributed by National Book Network

British Library Cataloguing in Publication Information Available

Library of Congress Cataloging-in-Publication Data

Ballard, Michael B.
U. S. Grant : the making of a general, 1861–1863 / Michael B.
    Ballard.
        p. cm. — (American crisis series ; no. 17)
    Includes bibliographical references and index.
    ISBN 0-7425-4308-0 (alk. paper)
    1. Grant, Ulysses S. (Ulysses Simpson), 1822–1885—Military
leadership. 2. Command of troops—History—19th century.
3. United States—History—Civil War, 1861–1865—Campaigns. 4.
Vicksburg (Miss.)—History—Siege, 1863. 5. Mississippi—History—
Civil War, 1861–1865. 6. Tennessee—History—Civil War, 1861–1865.
7. Generals—United States—Biography. I. Title. II. Series.
E672 .B34 2004
973.7'3'092—dc22

                                                                2003023983

Printed in the United States of America

♾ ™ The paper used in this publication meets the minimum requirements
of American National Standard for Information Sciences—Permanence of
Paper for Printed Library Materials, ANSI/NISO Z39.48-1992.

For

John F. Marszalek

as steadfast a friend, mentor, and colleague

as U. S. Grant was a soldier

ABOUT THE AUTHOR

Michael B. Ballard is a native of Ackerman, Mississippi, where he lives with his wife, Jan. He received both his M.A. and Ph.D. in history from Mississippi State University. He has worked for twenty years in the libraries at MSU, where he is currently a professor and University Archivist and Coordinator of the Congressional and Political Research Center. His books include *A Long Shadow: Jefferson Davis and the Final Days of the Confederacy* (1986), a History Book Club Selection; *Landscapes of Battle: The Civil War*, with David Muench (1988); *Pemberton: A Biography* (1991), a History Book Club Selection; *A Mississippi Rebel in the Army of Northern Virginia: The Civil War Memoirs of Private David Holt*, coedited with Thomas D. Cockrell (1995); and *Civil War Mississippi: A Guide* (2000).

CONTENTS

FOREWORD

When my friend, Steve Woodworth, asked if I would be interested in contributing to the American Crisis Series, I did not hesitate to accept. At the time I was in the midst of a project on the Vicksburg campaign, and Ulysses S. Grant—the man and the soldier—increasingly fascinated me. Among many works published about Grant, only one has focused specifically on his generalship: J. F. C. Fuller, *The Generalship of Ulysses S. Grant*, 1929, reprinted in 1958 by the University of Indiana Press. Some of Fuller's observations are still valid, but the evolution of Grant and Civil War historiography has passed them by. Biographers have, of course, addressed Grant's leadership abilities, but I thought that a slim study focusing on specific points of his development as a commander would be helpful to those who want a lean look at Grant, the general. I hope that this volume will make readers' further exploration of Grant in the several excellent biographies available a more meaningful experience.

I chose to focus on the years from 1861 to 1863 because I am convinced that Grant's experiences during this period molded him into the Union's most significant commander. He entered the war barely known beyond his cadre of West Point acquaintances, and yet by the end of 1863 he was the most recognized and most talked-about general in the Union army. It is my belief that his growth as a leader, both on the battlefield and in the world of military politics, occurred during his long trek from Belmont, Missouri, to Chattanooga, Tennessee. When one begins to understand the military Grant of the western theater, one better understands Grant the man.

Therefore, I have analyzed the positive and negative aspects of Grant's generalship at the battles of Belmont, Fort Henry and Fort Donelson, Shiloh, and Iuka. From Iuka I follow him through Earl Van Dorn's Corinth campaign (during which Grant did not exercise field command) and into the multifaceted Vicksburg campaign. Capturing Vicksburg, which sits high above the Mississippi River in west central Mississippi, proved to be a daunting challenge for Grant and the Union, and it took from November 1862 to July 1863 to succeed. The Vicksburg campaign demonstrates the numerous shades of Grant's character and leadership qualities more clearly

than any other military operation before or after. Forcing the surrender of the so-called Gibraltar of the Confederacy assured Grant
a prominent place in the history of the war. He topped that achievement by breaking the siege of Chattanooga and permanently driving Confederates out of that key Tennessee town. From that point,
he assumed command of all Union armies and in 1864–65 led the
Army of the Potomac to victory in Virginia. Grant's years in the
western theater molded him into the confident general who produced Union triumph in the East.

In putting together my interpretations of Grant, I have relied
on both my own observations and a synthesis of ideas that I have
absorbed through many years of studying the works of other schol-
ars. This book is not intended to be a full biography of Grant's war
years in the West. Rather, I have selected and analyzed certain aspects of his evolution as the Union's greatest general, aspects that I
think are essential to providing a clear picture of how this low-key,
practically unknown native of Ohio and then resident of Illinois
managed to ascend to the top of his profession and become a national hero and, ultimately, the eighteenth president of the United
States.

My approach has been to allow Grant to speak for himself. His
memoirs have been rightly praised as remarkably honest and insightful, and I have relied heavily on them. Grant's published papers and the official records of the war provide details of greater
immediacy of events that shaped the course of his generalship. I
believe that his qualities still have much to teach our generation
and those to come about the kinds of traits that produce success,
whether in military leadership or in other vocations. The most important Grant legacy is that he rarely complained, was unrelent-
ing, and just kept on keeping on, even during times of extraordinary
stress. His resilience, determination, humility, and refusal to accept anything short of victory are qualities that continue to make
him an appealing historical figure. Sam Grant was the kind of human being that made people feel comfortable, in spite of his rise to
fame and power. He still feels comfortable to the generations who
have followed, and we will never tire of studying his life.

Several special individuals contributed to the completion
of this book. John Marszalek, Steve Woodworth, and Terry Winschel
read the manuscript and offered valuable suggestions. Through the
years I have discussed the western theater, in general, and Grant,

in particular, with Marszalek, Winschel, Woodworth, Parker Hills, Ed Bearss, and Warren Graubau, and from those conversations have come many varying and fascinating perceptions of Grant. All these talented historians have influenced my thinking about him, and my views of the general have evolved from our discussions as well as from my research. We have not always agreed, but we have shared wonderful, memorable times exchanging ideas. I must emphasize, however, that the interpretations presented herein do not necessarily reflect the opinions of my friends. In addition, I am grateful for improvements in the narrative that are due to the considerable copyediting skills of Pat Sterling.

I also thank the love of my life, my beautiful bride, Jan, who is a skilled proofreader and constructive critic. She is an Illinois native who finds Grant an intriguing historical character and therefore enjoyed reviewing several versions of my manuscript; her suggestions were always beneficial. More than anything else, I appreciate her constant encouragement.

LIST OF MAPS

CHAPTER ONE

TRAINING GROUNDS

LOOKING BACK TO his arrival at the United States Military Academy as a student, Ulysses S. Grant admitted, "A military life had no charms for me, and I had not the faintest idea of staying in the army even if I should be graduated, which I did not expect." But he did graduate and survived many highs and lows to become one of his country's greatest military heroes and a two-term president. He traveled a bumpy road to fame, but the quiet, unassuming Ohioan time and again met and passed tests of patience and leadership. En route, he fulfilled the adage that success requires a man to get up one more time than he is knocked down. Fate, good fortune, or determination—more likely, a combination of all three—enabled Grant to bounce back, though during some particularly dark days he doubted he could keep going.[1]

Born Hiram Ulysses Grant on April 27, 1822, at Point Pleasant in southeastern Ohio, he grew into young manhood in nearby Georgetown, where his family moved shortly after his birth. His most notable attributes as a youngster were his skill on horseback and his tenacity, traits he retained for most of his life. When the time came for Ulysses to move beyond local educational opportunities, his father managed an appointment for him to West Point, picturesquely situated on Hudson River bluffs north of the city of New York. Young Grant might otherwise have accepted a farmer's life, though he admitted that at the time he "did not like to work," and successful farming required intense labor. More likely, he would have preferred employment on the Ohio River, which he had prowled extensively to the west, venting his ever present restlessness. His father wanted something more for him. The elder Grant did not necessarily envision a military career for his son, but he did think that the military academy's highly challenging engineering curriculum would provide significant career opportunities. This tendency to dominate and influence Ulysses created much tension between father and son. Though Grant spent many agonizing years trying to please his father, he came to resent the parental meddling that disrupted his efforts to lead his own life.[2]

Grant later observed, "I really had no objection to going to West Point, except that I had a very exalted idea of the acquirements necessary to get through. I did not believe I possessed them, and could not bear the idea of failing." Yet he could not bear to disappoint his father, and he "had always had a great desire to travel." He had already journeyed "east to Wheeling, Virginia [now West Virginia], and north to the Western Reserve, in Ohio, west to Louisville, and south to Bourbon County, Kentucky, besides having driven or ridden pretty much over the whole country within fifty miles of home." Now he would see more new country while traveling to New York. A military career usually demanded moving around, often to distant places, suiting Grant's restless nature.[3]

West Point meant more than new vistas; a paperwork error revised Grant's name. The Ohio congressman who appointed him, Thomas Hamer, assumed that Ulysses was Grant's first name, since that was what everyone called him, and placed an "S" for the middle initial, apparently believing that "S" stood for Simpson, Grant's mother's maiden name. Rather than fight red tape, Grant let the mistake stand and thus became Ulysses Simpson Grant, with the fateful initials U. S. He had never used "Hiram" anyway (except occasionally the "H" as a middle initial), and, in any event, the nickname "Sam," which he acquired at the Point, made the issue inconsequential.[4]

At West Point, Grant did not excel in the classroom other than in mathematics. Admittedly, he spent much of his time reading novels, "not those of a trashy sort" but books by such reputable authors as Washington Irving and Edward Bulwer-Lytton. He impressed many fellow cadets and visitors to the academy with his expert horsemanship, but otherwise he did not leave a major imprint on the memories of those he encountered. Although liked well enough, he lived a lone-wolf sort of existence, choosing to observe those around him, consciously or unconsciously evaluating their strengths and weaknesses, rather than developing intimate friendships. His propensity to study people served him in later years, when he had to size up enemy officers. Unfortunately, he was better at judging enemies than comrades in arms.

His thoughtful powers of observation impressed few; in fact, there was little about him that made fellow cadets think he would ever amount to much. When he eventually became a famous gen-

eral and a president, they struggled to remember something, anything, special about this quiet man they had known at the Point,
and they rarely could. They had not realized that despite his soli-
tude, Grant was absorbing the world around him, not merely glanc-
ing at it as it flowed by. He saw and felt more than he acknowledged,
and if his ego was not noticeably inflated, it nevertheless drove
him to dream of moving up the ladder of success. He remembered
the day that General Winfield Scott came to visit the academy, when
he, like most observers, was impressed by Scott's gaudy demeanor
(he lived up to his nickname, "Old Fuss and Feathers"). Grant knew
that he could never strut and wear such costumes, but he did imag-
ine returning to West Point some day and receiving the same sort
of attention as Scott.[5]

Grant and his fellow cadets learned the basics of army drill and
regulations, and these routines, which may have seemed boring at
the time, remained with many of them. They absorbed more than
they suspected, and the lessons paid dividends later when they
had to show citizen-soldiers how to handle firearms, how to fight,
and especially how to follow orders.

It was also at West Point that Grant met Julia, the sister of his
senior roommate, Frederick Dent. After Grant graduated in 1843,
ranked twenty-one out of thirty-nine, he and Dent were mustered
into the Fourth Infantry Regiment and assigned to Jefferson Bar-
racks in St. Louis, close to the Dents' home. On one occasion, when
he was riding horseback to see Julia before his unit left St. Louis
for Louisiana, Grant found a creek swollen by recent rains barring
his path. He recalled, "I looked at it a moment to consider what to
do. One of my superstitions had always been when I started to go
any where, or to do anything, not to turn back, or stop until the
thing intended was accomplished." So he urged the horse into the
stream, and they emerged soaking wet on the opposite bank. His
prideful account relates a significant truth about himself: his ego
might not be self-evident, but it was strong beneath the surface.[6]

Grant's feelings for Julia Dent grew quickly, and she recipro-
cated, but their wedding plans had to wait while he served in western Louisiana and then south Texas. Soon he went even farther, for
war loomed with Mexico. Meeting Julia was a turning point for
Grant, not only for the obvious reasons that he would someday
marry her and take on the responsibilities of husband and father
but also because his devotion to her made his future service in distant places much more difficult to handle. He still loved travel, but

he detested being away from his beloved Julia. His longing for her brought on depression, and he sought solace in a liquid antidote for which his body had little tolerance. In the process, he gained a reputation that haunted much of the rest of his life.[7]

U. S. Grant did not embrace the Mexican War as a great, noble American cause, but he and many other officers realized in later years that the conflict had taught them valuable lessons about leadership and about themselves. The classroom and the summer encampments at West Point had been intended to prepare cadets for war, but reaction to enemy fire often illuminated a man's soldierly qualities more accurately than classroom performance. Grant came out of Mexico convinced that he could endure war as well as anyone, but like most commonsense soldiers he did not consider it a romantic experience.[8]

Grant's aversion to political machinations also played a key role in his attitude toward the war. "For myself," he later wrote, "I was bitterly opposed to the measure [the declaration of war against Mexico], and to this day regard the war, which resulted, as one of the most unjust ever waged by a stronger against a weaker nation. It was an instance of a republic following the bad example of European monarchies, in not considering justice in their desire to acquire additional territory." He was reflecting not only on the war with Mexico but also on the ramifications of the controversy that it engendered: whether the territory won should be slave or free. He understood the theory of manifest destiny—that America was destined to stretch from ocean to ocean—and recognized that to many Americans the land gained "was an empire and of incalculable value; but it might have been obtained by other means. The Southern rebellion was largely the outgrowth of the Mexican war. Nations, like individuals, are punished for their transgressions. We got our punishment in the most sanguinary and expensive war of modern times." To Grant, the prize was not worth the cost. He may never have been a great intellectual, but he understood the basics of politics and the military. His words illustrate his distaste of political maneuvers that resulted in war, but his participation in both the Mexican conflict and the Civil War underscored his devotion to duty and his willingness to carry out his obligations as he saw them. Even in distasteful circumstances, he did not turn away.[9]

In Mexico, Grant learned much about himself as well as lessons from observing others. To his surprise, he remained calm under fire and experienced the unexpected adrenaline rush produced by the excitement of battle. His assignments varied, from leading a small infantry unit to serving as quartermaster of the Fourth Infantry. His horsemanship stood him in good stead on occasion, and he learned the value, and problems, of logistical support for an army in the field. He saw that in battle situations, maneuver often worked better than frontal assault, especially if a commander cared about holding down casualties. He met several former West Pointers—including his future Vicksburg campaign opponent, John C. Pemberton—and saw familiar faces, though whether he consciously evaluated their performances is unknown. Certainly he drew upon recollections of their characteristics when he encountered Mexican War officers as opponents in the Civil War.[10]

Grant absorbed the styles and methods of two generals in particular, Zachary Taylor and Winfield Scott. He liked Taylor's efforts to prohibit plundering on the part of his soldiers, and admired the way he shouldered pressure and responsibility when leading the first American troops into combat with Mexican forces in battles at Palo Alto and Resaca de la Palma in the summer of 1846. Grant also endorsed Taylor's rustic, frontier style: "General Taylor never made any great show or parade, either of uniform or retinue. In dress he was possibly too plain, rarely wearing anything in the field to indicate his rank, or even that he was an officer; but he was known to every soldier in his army, and was respected by all." Grant could relate to Taylor, noting further: "Taylor was not a conversationalist, but on paper he could put his meaning so plainly that there could be no mistaking it. He knew how to express what he wanted to say in the fewest well-chosen words, but would not sacrifice meaning to the construction of high-sounding sentences." General Grant wrote in a similar style.[11]

Though he was more comfortable with Taylor's style, Grant also found Scott an effective leader. He criticized some of Scott's tactics during the Mexico City campaign yet conceded that "General Scott's successes are an answer to all criticism. He invaded a populous country, penetrating two hundred and sixty miles into the interior, with a force at no time equal to one-half of that opposed to him; he was without a base; the enemy was always intrenched [sic], always on the defensive; yet he won every battle, he captured the capital, and conquered the government. Credit is due to the troops engaged, it is true, but the plans and the strategy were the general's." In effect, Grant observed that good generalship, no matter the style, made the difference. Results counted more than method, and

General Grant believed that if going by the book did not work, then he would write his own when it came to managing campaigns and battles.[12]

There was no doubt about his personal preference between Taylor and Scott: "Both were true, patriotic and upright in all their dealings. Both were pleasant to serve under—Taylor was pleasant to serve with. Scott saw more through the eyes of his staff officers than through his own. His plans were deliberately prepared, and fully expressed in orders. Taylor saw for himself, and gave orders to meet the emergency without reference to how they would read in history." Grant, too, would be his own general, because he did not believe in abdicating the job to a staff, and he would do whatever was necessary to win, no matter the obstacles. Taylor had bred a disciple.[13]

Grant's mention that Scott had no supply base is interesting in light of his future insistence that he also gave up his base during the Vicksburg campaign. Scott did have a supply base in the Vera Cruz area, and although his connection to it was often tenuous, supplies did make their way by wagon and pack mule to his army as it marched inland toward Mexico City. Similarly, Grant drew supplies from a base at Grand Gulf on the Mississippi River during the early inland phase of his May 1863 campaign against Vicksburg. Grant's interpretation of the two situations is misleading, but it is apparent that he took his later cue from Scott's campaign.[14]

Grant did not fully appreciate all he had learned and experienced in Mexico until secession led to hostilities between Americans in 1861. When the Mexican War ended, he relished peace, and after accompanying his regiment to Pascagoula, Mississippi, on the Gulf of Mexico, he secured leave, traveled up the Mississippi to St. Louis, and married Julia Dent on August 22, 1848. Following a brief honeymoon, during which the couple visited Grant's Ohio home, he began a long odyssey of service in varied locales: New York, Michigan, and back to New York to travel with his regiment— mostly by ocean, Atlantic to Pacific—to new duties on the West Coast. There he served as regimental quartermaster, first in San Francisco and then in Oregon Territory.[15]

Like many officers, Grant hoped to supplement his income in order to bring Julia and their growing family west. But everything he tried—from potato farming to woodcutting to hiring out horses to selling chickens and cattle—failed, and Grant, already despondent at being separated from Julia, became increasingly depressed. To numb the pain he turned to whiskey, and it quickly became apparent that a little alcohol was too much for him. He had sworn off drinking at West Point after seeing another cadet in a drunken stupor, but loneliness overwhelmed his resolve. His brief, rare episodes with liquor laid the groundwork for the gossip and innuendo that dogged him for many years. Grant could never have anticipated that tales of his adventures with the bottle would be so blown out of proportion by those who sought to discredit him. Of course, he had no way of knowing that he would become so prominent a figure as to turn any questionable behavior into fodder for gossips. Enemies, rivals, and even friends would often explain a fall or an illness by alluding to Grant's problems handling alcohol. It took only a few grains of truth to build mountains of suspicion.

When he decided to give up military life, word immediately spread that he had been asked to resign to avoid a court-martial for out-of-control drinking. No evidence exists to support such charges, and one of Grant's biographers is doubtless accurate in asserting that "Grant did not leave the army because he was a drunk. He drank and left the army because he was profoundly depressed"—as did other West Pointers. Grant himself never alluded to drinking problems as a cause of his resignation. In his memoir he wrote simply, "My family, all this while, was at the East. It consisted now of a wife and two children. I saw no chance of supporting them on the Pacific coast out of my pay as an army officer. I concluded, therefore, to resign, and in March [1854] applied for a leave of absence until the end of the July following, tendering my resignation to take effect at the end of that time."[16]

Once he was home, Grant's family and Julia's pressured him to decide between two very different career choices. His father wanted him to go to work in a family business, a general store that his two brothers operated in Galena, in the northwestern corner of Illinois; Julia's father offered him farmland near the Dent home in St. Louis. He made his decision when he learned that his father expected Julia and the children to stay with the Grant family in its new location at Covington, Kentucky, while Ulysses worked in Galena. Rebuffing this latest attempt by his father to manipulate his life, and remembering his painful loneliness out west, Grant rejected Galena. He would farm in St. Louis and be with his wife and children.

Thus, in 1855, the former soldier was toiling in the fields alongside slaves owned by the Dents. His crop production was respectable, but fluctuating sale prices prevented a decent, steady income, and Grant resorted to cutting and selling firewood to bring in extra money. When he decided to build a home for his family, the result was a rough-looking cabin that he dubbed "Hardscrabble"—a fitting name. The Grants lived there only a short time, however, because Julia, accustomed to finer surroundings, did not like the place. When her mother died, her father invited the family to live in a nearby Dent property called White Haven. Soon, Grant was overseeing Dent operations, but he found it difficult to supervise large numbers of slaves; he did not reject slavery out of hand, but he was made uncomfortable by its proximity. Like many midwesterners with Democratic Party leanings, he believed that the North should not interfere with slaveholding, and he worried that continued tension could lead to slave uprisings in the South. He thought that slavery was a dying institution and that patience might be the best means of avoiding war.

Grant had little time to dwell on politics, however, for the Panic of 1857 hit his farming operations hard, forcing him to expand his woodcutting sideline. His father, always reluctant to help except on his own terms, assured his son that he could expect no Grant family financial assistance as long as he lived among slaveholders. Hence, an increasingly desperate Ulysses gave in to his father's offer to work in family enterprises in Covington. It was a move Julia strongly opposed, and her resistance eventually brought the family back to St. Louis. Grant wound up working with one of her cousins, collecting rental fees and other debts. Julia knew that her husband was too gentle a soul to make it in a business that required toughness.

Occasionally racked with malarial fever attacks and accompanying chills, Grant drifted as he searched for his niche in life. Again out of desperation to remain solvent, he accepted his father's offer to go to Galena, this time with his family, and work his way into the business there. They traveled upriver in April 1860 to the beautiful little Illinois town on the Mississippi River, where Grant continued to struggle in the business world and subsequently incurred many debts. He nevertheless seemed content, even amid the continual roar of national political division over slavery. Hoping that the Democrats could keep a lid on this issue that was tearing the country apart, he had voted for James Buchanan in 1856. Now he tried to stay above the fray as the 1860 presidential election approached, but he dreaded the effect that victory by Republican

Abraham Lincoln might have on the country. Since he was not yet a legal resident of Illinois, he could not go to the polls but it appears that had he been eligible, he would have voted for Democrat Stephen A. Douglas.[17]

As the threat of war loomed, Grant had no idea what his future held. His pre–Civil War years had demonstrated his staying power, stubbornness, and resolve to move ahead no matter what the obstacles. He had made it through West Point with persistence, not flash. His military career had been a learning experience and an endurance trial, and he had shown he could both lead and follow. The uncertain warrior had proved tough under fire and had learned what it took to feed and supply a large army. He had observed effective commanders and the success of low-key generalship. He had suffered disappointments, especially being away from his wife and children, and then several years of tough economic times in the struggle to succeed as the breadwinner for a growing family. Yet through it all, he kept pushing ahead; when one venture failed, he tried another. And he did not seem to mind the whispers and finger-pointing engendered by his failures or his marriage to a woman from a slaveholding family. Determined, resilient, and persistent, Ulysses Grant would soon need those qualities more than he could ever have imagined.

NOTES

1. Ulysses S. Grant, *Personal Memoirs of U. S. Grant: Selected Letters, 1839–1865*, 2 vols. in one (New York, 1990), 31.
2. Ibid., 27; Brooks D. Simpson, *Ulysses S. Grant: Years of Adversity, 1822–1865* (Boston, 2000), 4, 5, 9, 14; William S. McFeely, *Grant: A Biography* (New York, 1981), 11–12.
3. Grant, *Memoirs*, 28–29.
4. Simpson, *Grant*, 11–12; McFeely, *Grant*, 13–14.
5. Grant, *Memoirs*, 32–33; Simpson, *Grant*, 16–17; McFeely, *Grant*, 20.
6. Grant, *Memoirs*, 38; Simpson, *Grant*, 18; McFeely, *Grant*, 20.
7. Simpson, *Grant*, 27; McFeely, *Grant*, 26–27; Grant, *Memoirs*, 39.
8. Grant, *Memoirs*, 41.
9. Ibid., 41–42.
10. Ibid., 109, 129; Simpson, *Grant*, 32–33, 35, 45–46; McFeely, *Grant*, 33, 37.
11. Grant, *Memoirs*, 70, 95; McFeely, *Grant*, 38.
12. Grant, *Memoirs*, 113.
13. Ibid., 95.
14. Ibid., 328; John Edward Weems, *To Conquer a Peace: The War between the United States and Mexico* (College Station, TX, 1988), 357, 379, 390.

15. Grant, *Memoirs*, 130–39 passim.

16. Ibid., 141; Simpson, *Grant*, 14, 44–45, 58, 61; McFeely, *Grant*, 55.

17. Simpson, *Grant*, 63–77, 79, 82; Grant, *Memoirs*, 141–51; McFeely, *Grant*, 58–70.

CHAPTER TWO

BELMONT

U. S. GRANT'S ENTRY into the Civil War in 1861 held little hint of what was to come. He presided at a pro-Union town meeting in Galena and helped train a local company of volunteers. He traveled with these citizen-soldiers to the state capital at Springfield and, at the request of Governor Richard Yates, worked in the state adjutant general's office, where his quartermaster experience helped him manage seemingly endless paperwork. John Pope, an acquaintance from his military days, offered to recommend Grant for a command position, but Grant politely refused; he wanted to be appointed on his own merit rather than through someone else's influence. A personal letter to Washington, where the War Department had been swamped by requests for commissions, possibly got lost; in any event, Grant received no response. But he had spent enough time in the army to understand that he who did nothing received nothing. So he traveled to Kentucky, ostensibly to visit his parents but certainly with the hope of seeing George McClellan —newly commanding the Department of the Ohio—and perhaps obtaining a position on his staff. He never met with McClellan, but after Governor Yates appointed him colonel of the Twenty-first Illinois, he did meet two future officers he would get to know well. John McClernand and John Logan, both pro-Union Illinois Democrats and members of the U.S. House of Representatives, arrived in Springfield and asked to address his troops. Grant agreed, unaware of how much of his future would be associated with these men.

Grant led his regiment into south central Illinois and later to Missouri, hither and yon, searching for Rebel troops. The Confederates were burning bridges and raiding Union supplies, and Grant intended to drive them out. At one point, he recalled that when marching his men toward a reported Confederate camp in Missouri, "I would have given anything then to have been back in Illinois, but I had not the moral courage to halt and consider what to do; I kept right on. When we reached a point from which the valley below was in full view I halted." The enemy camp had been abandoned, so his "heart resumed its place." That the Rebels feared him as much as he dreaded them was a revelation that eased future anxieties. His observation showed that he was the kind of commander who looked for an edge over his opponents, which he had gained on this occasion by simply moving against them. Active armies and an active mind came to characterize Grant's generalship. His propensity to do his job, despite misgivings, was obvious, as was his tendency to learn from experiences, even in operations that produced insignificant results.[1]

During his odyssey in search of Rebel guerrillas, which accomplished little more than getting troops used to marching, camping, and drilling, Grant heard that the Illinois congressional delegation had included his name on a list sent to the president for promotion to brigadier general. He suspected that his politically influential friend, the Illinois congressman Elihu Washburne, was behind the inclusion of his name, and he was right. Grant got the appointment and quickly began putting together a staff. He sought men he trusted, and the list included John Rawlins, a close friend from Galena, who, after his wife's death, joined Grant in September and remained with him as a staff officer and confidant throughout the war.

General Grant's first assignment took him to Ironton, Missouri, where he set up headquarters. He commanded the district around Ironton, located some seventy miles south of St. Louis. Farther south, William J. Hardee's Confederate troops were camped at Greenville. As Grant prepared to go after Hardee, General Benjamin Prentiss arrived to take over the district, for Grant had been promoted to command a larger area that included most of central Missouri. Apparently, his ability to mold raw recruits into something resembling a fighting force had caught the attention of his superiors, especially John C. Fremont, in charge of the vaguely defined Department of the West. Grant's new assignment took him to Jefferson City, the Missouri capital. Union officials worried that Sterling Price, a well-known Missourian fighting for the Confederacy, might attack the place, and Grant's job was to bring order to the chaotic situation there, created by disorganized troops, and to defend the capital. Grant did well, noting simply in his memoirs, "Order was soon restored." He prepared for campaigning and then was relieved again, this time in favor of Jefferson C. Davis, a native of Indiana. Grant, somewhat mystified, proceeded to St. Louis, where "special instructions" awaited him.[2]

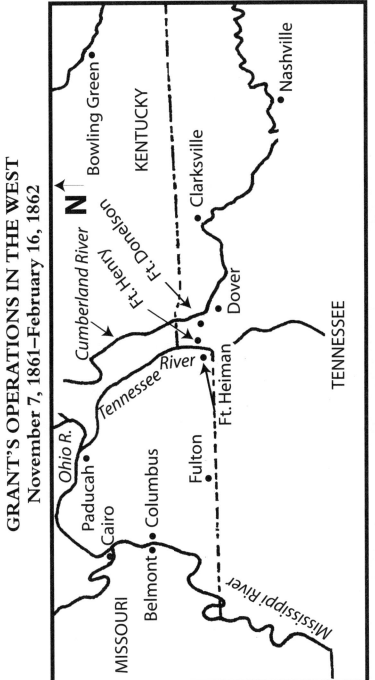

GRANT'S OPERATIONS IN THE WEST
November 7, 1861–February 16, 1862

Adapted from Benjamin Franklin Cooling, *Forts Henry and Donelson: The Key to the Confederate Heartland* (Knoxville: University of Tennessee Press, 1987), 13.

That transfer at least brought Grant the comfort of being close to his family and his darling Julia. In fact, Julia and their son Fred spent much time with the general during the next four years of conflict, and their presence no doubt eased the pressures of his multiple commands. No wonder he responded quickly to his latest orders: "In an hour after being relieved from the command I was on my way to St. Louis, leaving my single staff officer to follow the next day with our horses and baggage."[3]

Grant's new assignment made him commander of the District of Southeast Missouri, which included all of Missouri south of St. Louis as well as southern Illinois. His first specific assignment was to go after Jeff Thompson, a Rebel partisan commander. Grant established temporary headquarters in Cape Girardeau on the west bank of the Mississippi. He experienced a brief brush with the politics of command when Benjamin Prentiss rebelled at being placed under Grant's authority. Grant thought Prentiss's behavior ill advised, for it cost the latter promotions he might otherwise have gained. The military hierarchy frowned on officers with mutinous reputations; several of lower grade bypassed Prentiss. Beyond the problems he created for himself, Prentiss's action not only warned Grant to expect such aberrations when dealing with prideful men but also contributed to Thompson's escape. Grant noted that it did not matter, however, for "Thompson moved light and had no fixed place for even nominal headquarters. He was as much at home in Arkansas as he was in Missouri and would keep out of the way of a superior force." Grant understood that prioritizing his responsibilities kept him from wasting time chasing elusive guerrillas, who, in the end, usually caused more frustration than damage.[4]

Battlefield action seemed to evade him, and Grant well understood that being idle accomplished nothing either for him or for the Union cause. Memories of his prewar failures haunted him; Grant often felt burdened by his past, no matter how distant or recent. He seemed driven to prove something to himself and to Washington. On September 3, 1861, he moved his headquarters to Cairo, Illinois, where the Ohio River surged into the Mississippi. His was one of several forces expected to get the attention of General Leonidas Polk's Confederate army, which had occupied Columbus, Kentucky. Since Polk's advance to Columbus had violated Kentucky's shaky neutrality, Union officials had no compunction about attacking Rebels on Kentucky soil.[5]

At Cairo, Grant received reports that Confederates had moved toward Paducah, Kentucky, which lay on the Ohio River at the mouth of the Tennessee. Grant reported the news to his immediate superior, General Fremont, and then seized the initiative by stating his intent to lead an expedition to keep Paducah from falling into enemy hands. Hearing no objections from Fremont, who had earlier suggested the possible need to take Paducah, Grant occupied the town on September 6. His presence caused Polk to pull back to Columbus. He then reinforced his initial occupation forces and placed General Charles Ferguson Smith, a 54-year-old West Pointer whom he greatly admired, in local command. Returning to Cairo, he found a message from Fremont giving him permission to do what he had already done. The lesson was not lost on Grant; thereafter, he acted when he thought action the proper course, rather than sit around waiting for instructions or approval to make their way through the military's red tape. It could be risky business, but in wartime, politicians—whether civilian or military—whose careers depended on victory tended to cut aggressive generals some slack.[6]

Beginning his Civil War service in the West gave Grant more flexibility to exercise his own judgment in the field, for the wide expanse of the western theater forced commanders to leave much decision-making in the hands of subordinates. In the East, where the general area of operations was much more restricted and the federal government close by, his tendency to take the initiative without permission would not likely have been tolerated. The additional freedom that western commanders enjoyed both benefited Grant and caused him trouble, but overall, it facilitated his growing into the leader he became. Paducah gave him his first opportunity to act aggressively in the field without specific orders to do so, and he had gotten away with it. He no doubt concluded that his continual promotion upward into more responsible jobs meant that his superiors trusted him to take care of things, and with that growth of confidence came a belief in his ability to make the right decisions.

Having occupied a town where Union loyalty was not necessarily predominant, Grant calmed the fear and consternation among Paducah citizens by proclaiming to them "our peaceful intentions, that we had come among them to protect them against the enemies of our country, and that all who chose could continue their usual avocations with assurance of the protection of the government."

Grant's approach became one of his trademarks in dealing with Confederate sympathizers; he strongly believed that a soft touch would bring anti-Union people to their senses more quickly than harsh occupation policies. He found that such an approach produced only limited results, however, as the conflict wore on and Union strategy shifted toward one of hard war. He eventually came to understand that hard-line Confederates could not be easily appeased, if at all.[7]

Grant was aware of the unsettled political situation in Kentucky, where, early in the war, Union and Confederate partisans shared power in the state government. To cover himself, he took the liberty of informing the Kentucky legislature of his action at Paducah. The Unionist majority in that body approved, but Grant later was "reprimanded [by Fremont] for my correspondence with the legislature and warned against a repetition of that offence." Grant filed that lesson away and learned to act with a much more delicate touch in the wartime political arena.[8]

Nevertheless, the initiative Grant demonstrated during this period showed plainly that he had no intention of being a quiet, low-key leader. Those who saw Grant's style as being drab, like his clothing, underestimated his ego; a humble general would not occupy a town and communicate with a state legislature without permission. This was a proud man, eager to make a mark for himself. Even as he learned to play politics more deftly, he never shrank from taking a stand when he thought it necessary to do so.

In Paducah through the rest of September and all of October 1861, Grant's troops sat, drilled, and waited for orders and further developments along the Mississippi Valley. Finally, on November 1, Grant received a welcome message at his headquarters in Cairo from Fremont's St. Louis headquarters directing him "to hold your whole command ready to march at an hour's notice, until further orders, and you will take particular care to be amply supplied with transportation and ammunition. You are also directed to make demonstrations with your troops along both sides of the river towards Charleston, Norfolk, and Blandville [Kentucky], and to keep your columns constantly moving back and forward against these places, without, however, attacking the enemy." In effect, Grant's troops were to implement feinting and diversion, tactics that Grant came to embrace and perfect. It was not a call to battle, but he had something to do, and he used the experience to continue his never ending schooling in the art of effective warfare.[9]

As Grant prepared to coordinate his diversions with General Smith, a second message arrived detailing the presence of a Confederate force led by Jeff Thompson in southeastern Missouri. A Union detachment was en route to drive Thompson into Arkansas, and Grant was to send troops to assist. He responded without hesitation, ordering forward a detachment under R. J. Oglesby. He was advised to exercise caution, but, not satisfied with the goal of simply driving Thompson out of Missouri, Grant wrote to Oglesby: "The object of the expedition is to destroy this force, and the manner of doing it is left largely at your discretion, believing it better not to trammel you with instructions." He may have thought Thompson insignificant within the big picture, but Grant could not tolerate allowing this partisan to cause the diversion of troops needed elsewhere. Supplies would be sent, but Oglesby could impress additional food, though records must be kept and receipts given to citizens from whom goods were taken. Foraging was prohibited, for "it is demoralizing in the extreme, and is apt to make open enemies where they would not otherwise exist."[10]

In these instructions, Grant revealed two basic strategic concepts that remained with him throughout the war. First, he tended to leave tactical decisions to his subordinates. Grant was a planner; he could look at maps and see what must be done, but he preferred to let his officers carry out operations with as little hindrance from him as possible. Second, though he gradually changed his views on foraging, he believed firmly that his armies should not alienate citizens by heavy-handed confiscation of supplies.

When Grant received word that Sterling Price's Confederate army in Missouri was being reinforced from Columbus, Kentucky, he stepped up his own demonstrations designed to freeze, or at least slow, Confederate movements. He directed Oglesby to march toward New Madrid, Missouri, and sent a reinforcing detachment to Charleston, Missouri. Next, he directed Oglesby to move beyond New Madrid toward Columbus and open communications with Grant, who was himself leading a force to Belmont, located on the Missouri side of the Mississippi directly across from Columbus. W. H. L. Wallace, commanding at Bird's Point, Missouri, on the Mississippi across from and south of Cairo, was to join Oglesby. Grant also sent word to Smith at Paducah and to John Cook at Fort Holt, Kentucky, that they should demonstrate toward Columbus to keep the Confederates guessing and to prevent their sending reinforcements elsewhere. Throughout all this maneuvering, Grant gained experience in putting together complex operations designed to confuse the enemy.[11]

As Grant headed downriver toward Belmont, Oglesby closed on the same target. A portion of a column from Cape Girardeau was to check Thompson's operations and reinforce Grant at Belmont if necessary. Wallace merged half a regiment with Oglesby's troops; John Cook moved south; and two of Smith's columns, approaching Belmont from different directions, completed the varying Union movements. Grant's goal was to concentrate these scattered forces against Belmont, while at the same time throttling Jeff Thompson. It was a complex series of movements, but Grant, helped by a very able personal staff, managed to coordinate them quite well. These operations preceding a forthcoming fight at Belmont prepared Grant for greater challenges that he later met farther downriver.[12]

On November 6, Grant left Cairo, traveling with John McClernand's brigade of 3,100 men via transports down the Mississippi. The troop transports anchored on the Kentucky shore, for Grant intended to convince Rebels in Columbus that he had come to attack. Next morning, he allegedly received word from Wallace (a Grant claim denied by Wallace) of civilian intelligence indicating that Confederates had crossed the river to Belmont with the intent of attacking Oglesby. Grant later argued that he wanted to keep the Confederates from sending troops to Price and to prevent them from intercepting and assaulting Oglesby's column. There is evidence that he decided after the fact to add those intentions to his reasons for moving on Belmont; his messages before attacking the town reveal no such concerns. If he padded his report with rationales, he no doubt did so to convince Fremont that the campaign against Belmont had been fully justified. Whatever the case, Grant decided "to attack vigorously" the enemy forces at Belmont, "knowing that should we be repulsed, we would re-embark without difficulty under the protection of the gunboats."[13]

Three points are striking. First, Grant realized the significance of the Union navy along the Mississippi. As his Civil War career progressed, he often relied on naval assistance and power to carry out his campaign goals. Second, Grant was acting on questionable intelligence about a Confederate presence at Belmont. Since the source, a man supposedly loyal to the Union, might or might not be reliable, the sound move would have been to send trusted scouts to validate this news. Third, if Grant indeed falsified his battle report with unfounded reasons for having attacked at Belmont, he

UNION APPROACH AT BELMONT
November 7, 1861

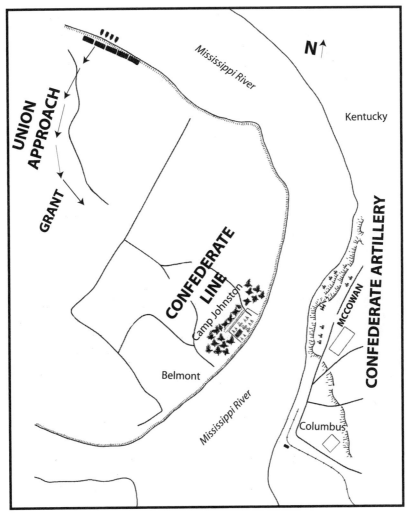

Adapted from Nathaniel C. Hughes Jr., *The Battle of Belmont: Grant Strikes South* (Chapel Hill: University of North Carolina Press, 1991), 80.

undoubtedly did so to protect himself from potential criticism. Aggressiveness was one thing, but reckless aggressiveness could damage a career. Although he had done what he thought was right, he understood that damage control might be necessary, and he had no compunction about covering his tracks.

Aboard the steamer *Belle Memphis* on November 7, Grant wrote attack orders. The troop transports would move out at 6:00 A.M., with gunboats in the lead. Grant's small force consisted of two brigades, the first comprising McClernand's three regiments from Cairo and Fort Holt; the second, two regiments led by Colonel Henry Dougherty—a total of some 3,100 men.[14]

Grant sought the advice of a pilot as the gunboats churned downstream. He wanted to know how close to Belmont the army could land and still be out of sight of Confederate troops in Columbus. He could not attack Belmont frontally from the river, for his forces and vessels would be caught in a crossfire between Rebels in the town on the west bank and the Confederate artillery known to be on the heights of Columbus along the river's east bank. The only feasible plan would be to land on the west bank north of Belmont and attack from west to east. The pilot answered that the best landing spot would be about three miles north of Belmont, and Grant nodded his approval, accepting without question the pilot's choice. In the future, U. S. Grant would insist on seeing things for himself, but his willingness to push forward on the word of a stranger underscored his desire to keep the operation moving.[15]

Grant counted on Henry Walke's naval flotilla to occupy Polk's guns along a ridge known as Iron Banks, which overlooked the river on the Kentucky side. Fog caused the cancellation of the initial attempt by two gunboats, the *Tyler* and the *Lexington*, to engage the Confederates before the army disembarked, but the landing came off without a hitch, and Grant led his army toward Belmont for about a mile before forming a battle line. While the army surged forward, the two Union gunboats again approached Columbus from the north and drew fire from Confederate batteries. The Federal vessels were well built but made of timber. (The ironclads that soon strengthened Union naval power were still under construction.) After a time, the boats withdrew.[16]

McClernand was told by Grant to send two companies forward from each brigade to ascertain Rebel positions. About 9:00 A.M. the skirmish line made contact with the Confederates, and Grant ordered the rest of his force, minus one battalion left behind at the river as a reserve, to advance. Judging from the difference in details between their reports and Grant's, McClernand and Henry Dougherty, who was wounded and captured during the battle, coordinated battle tactics—though McClernand's habitual braggadocio must be taken into account. Still, Grant himself applauded

McClernand's performance in a private letter written after the battle; he stated that the politician had proved himself as a soldier and exhibited a calm and courageous demeanor. McClernand and Dougherty also gave credit to their officers for maintaining formations that occasionally went awry. The major point is that the two brigade commanders' reports are filled with tactical details that are noticeably absent from Grant's; thus, there is no way of knowing just how much Grant may have contributed to battlefield decisions. He was certainly on the scene, but he likely allowed his commanders to direct maneuvers.[17]

Perhaps Grant understood that his greatest ability was as a strategist, not as a battlefield tactician. He could plan and direct, but once the shooting started, he seemed to believe that lower-level officers on the scene could make better decisions than one man who was trying to control the entirety of a battlefield. The danger of this approach could be a lack of coordination among troops scattered over a wide front, and Grant had not yet developed a staff who could assist him in keeping up with battlefield activities. As time passed, he became more comfortable issuing orders to subordinates during the fighting, but he did not dictate battlefield operations unless he saw the need to do so. As one of his biographers has noted, at Belmont he did little more than encourage his men, and his "staff officers functioned more as a headquarters escort than they did as instruments of command."[18]

McClernand kept up the pressure, employing a tactic that became his favorite. He believed in using his numbers to overwhelm, and Grant, though he would never say so, given the lukewarm feelings between the two and their later outright alienation, no doubt respected his subordinate's aggressiveness. Hard-charging Union troops forced Confederates from their initial position to their rear, toward the river.[19]

Grant watched as his men "drove the enemy foot by foot, and from tree to tree, back to his encampment on the river bank, a distance of over 2 miles." As the Confederate line fell back, Federal soldiers came within range of both Rebel field artillery and the big guns at Columbus. Shells shredded trees and fell among the charging Union troops. The infantry fighting became hotter, and McClernand received a jolt when a Confederate bullet hit his pistol holster, but the gun inside, though dented, saved the general from a flesh wound. Grant took a fall when his horse was shot out from under him. McClernand later wrote of Grant's presence with admiration, noting that the army's "gallant conduct was stimulated by your presence and inspired by your example."[20]

During the fighting, Union gunboats made a third appearance, having previously returned to swap fire with Confederate batteries for about twenty minutes. This time, Walke's boats shelled Camp Johnston, named in honor of Albert Sidney Johnston, who commanded all Confederate forces in the West. Though fortified with infantry and artillery and protected by heavy woods, the fort had been built as an observation post on the Missouri side of the river, for it lay on a plateau adjacent to the Mississippi. A Rebel shell struck the *Tyler*, Walke's vessel, beheading one man and injuring two others. The shot seemed to unnerve Walke, and the boats backed upstream and returned to the embarkation point. As a result the boats were not present to keep Polk from sending reinforcements across the river to Gideon J. Pillow, who commanded a division under Polk. Grant discovered that a successful commander must be ready to make adjustments to his plans when factors he has counted on, in this case gunboat assistance, fail to materialize.[21]

The Federal push frequently encountered obstructions of brush and felled trees, some of which were arranged near Camp Johnston as abatis (sharpened poles positioned to point toward the enemy), but the men forced their way through such obstructions throughout the battle and drove the Rebels back into Belmont. Pillow, who had arrived not long before with five regiments, urged his soldiers on to stop the Union wave, but Federal troops pressed the Confederate center and both flanks, forcing Pillow's withdrawal through cornfields to Camp Johnston. Though Grant may not have been on the scene directing troop operations, flank attacks became one of the trademarks of his battle philosophy of misdirection. His troops carried out his strategic design and desire through their tactical maneuvers, indicating that Grant and his subordinates had talked and planned together. Grant appreciated the necessity of planning and teamwork in executing troop movements and no doubt promoted the concept among his lieutenants.

The fight dragged on, with Pillow begging Polk for reinforcements that did not come, largely because, Polk said, he feared an attack directly on Columbus by other Union forces that Grant had ordered to wait close by. Though he probably had more troops in action on the battlefield than Grant, Pillow's ammunition ran low; he ordered a countercharge, but to no avail. Finally, he pulled back to the river, where Pillow found one Rebel regiment disembarking;

though he formed for a counterattack, he knew that help had come too late. The lack of Confederate coordination demonstrated just how successful Grant's aggressive surprise move had been and how fortunate he was to be going against enemy generals of, at best, mediocre ability.[22]

Federals ransacked and wrecked abandoned Confederate camps, and McClernand, who had another narrow escape when a minié ball grazed his head, called for "three cheers for the Union." He sent artillery to fire at Confederate boats and at the Columbus heights, while Grant, who did not have wagons to haul off booty and knew he could not occupy Belmont as long as Confederate artillery sat on the bluffs across the Mississippi, ordered the soldiers to set ablaze enemy tents and other camp equipage. At this point, Pillow sent three fresh Confederate regiments, led by Benjamin Cheatham, from upriver toward Grant's left in an attempt to flank the Federals and cut off their retreat route. Grant worried that some of his men, not yet used to combat, would be ready to give up when cries of "surrounded" rang out, but once he "announced that we had cut our way in and could cut our way out just as well," the men formed and marched back toward their transports. Some hard fighting did occur, but McClernand's troops kept the Rebels at bay.[23]

Grant later complained about the lack of discipline among many of his troops and officers. "The moment the [Confederate] camp was reached," he wrote, "our men laid down their arms and commenced rummaging the tents to pick up trophies. Some of the higher officers were little better than the privates. They galloped about from one cluster of men to another and at every halt delivered a short eulogy upon the Union cause and the achievements of command." These words from Grant's memoirs reveal a thinly veiled criticism of McClernand, whose speechmaking always annoyed him.[24]

In fact, Lincoln, ever mindful of keeping fellow politicians happy, later wrote McClernand to congratulate him on his performance at Belmont; Grant received no such letter. McClernand wrote the president after the fight to report on the needs of the western army, and Lincoln, responding that the government was doing the best it could to get arms and supplies to all Union forces, asked for patience. The correspondence is a clear indication that McClernand would not hesitate to contact Washington directly and take advantage of his influence with Lincoln. He wanted to be remembered, for no doubt he already envisioned some sort of independent command that would provide better chances for glory—ambitions that made Grant's future tasks more difficult. By contrast, John Logan, another Illinois politician in uniform who also performed admirably at Belmont, became Grant's staunch ally in coming campaigns. Other officers had also done well; in this first test of a Grant team on the battlefield, the commanding general had reason to be pleased.[25]

The Federal army retraced its steps, taking along confiscated artillery, several enemy horses, and a few prisoners. The return march to the river soon grew dangerous, as Confederates kept appearing and reappearing ahead, attempting to block the army from reaching the transports; McClernand later recalled his men "driving the enemy back on either side." Seizing the moment, Grant ordered a charge; his infantry chased away the enemy "and again defeated him." With the exception of one Illinois regiment, which had taken a wrong, roundabout road back to the landing, Union troops reached their transports and boarded without further problems.[26]

As the boats sat waiting for the missing regiment, work details loaded the wounded, who were moved from makeshift field hospitals. Grant rode in search of a guard he had posted but did not find the men and learned eventually that their commander had sent them back to the boats with the rest of the troops. Deciding not to reverse the order, Grant rode on alone to survey the landscape in the direction of the expected Confederate pursuit but saw nothing until he suddenly spotted what proved to be enemy troops some fifty yards away. At a later truce conference with Polk, Grant learned that enemy soldiers had been given permission to shoot at him, but none did.[27]

By this time, more Confederates indeed had crossed the Mississippi from Columbus and fired on the transports. A general battle broke out, with Union gunboats pitching in to help Grant's army. (The few Illinoisans still trying to reach the landing would eventually be picked up along the river.) The "terrible fire of the gunboats" felled many Confederates, or at least seemed to, and ended what had been a six-hour fight. Reported casualties were actually few among the Rebels along the bank; some of the effect noted by Union soldiers may have been enemy soldiers diving to the ground to avoid exploding shells. In any event, the Confederates retreated, and all the Union forces made good their withdrawal. Grant in his memoirs uncharacteristically, and very likely accurately, dramatized his own escape, claiming to be the last man aboard, crediting his horse (and by implication his horsemanship) with sliding down the riverbank and boarding "over a single gang plank." Once aboard the *Belle Memphis*, Grant went into the captain's quarters and tumbled onto a sofa for a moment before getting up to go out on deck. As he walked away, a bullet hit "the head of the sofa, passed through it and lodged in the foot."[28]

Grant reported his losses as 85 killed, 301 wounded, and 99 missing; he estimated that of his wounded, 125 had fallen into Confederate hands. He praised his troops and officers for their "gallantry" and "coolness" in addition to singling out McClernand and Dougherty for the quality of their leadership. The Confederates had 642 combined casualties. As usual in battle reports, each side gave the other credit for many more men than it actually had. In truth, the opposing armies were of nearly equal numbers, with a slight edge to the Confederates, as each side fielded between 2,500 and 3,000 men during the main fighting at Belmont. The total number of Confederates engaged was around 5,000, but the Federals did not encounter them all at once.[29]

Grant, who had seen many dead and wounded in Mexico, still regretted his losses, even though as a seasoned soldier he understood that war necessarily produced casualties. Although he eventually cultivated a close relationship with the men in the ranks, at Belmont he had a rocky beginning. In the aftermath, one officer noted that Grant seemed cold and unfeeling but added that the difference between the general and the inexperienced soldiers he commanded was that he was "a *real* soldier," not an "amateur." Some soldiers did not think that Grant fought wisely, that he needlessly sacrificed lives in reckless attacks, yet many came to his, and their own, defense when Northern newspapers disparaged the Federal effort at Belmont. Grant and his men continued to grow toward each other. He may not have been an inspirational, physical presence among his troops at Belmont; over time, however, he instilled confidence in those who followed him by leading them to victories.

In other campaign action, Oglesby's expedition never corralled Jeff Thompson; in the end, his troops marched many miles and accomplished nothing. Smith's demonstration from Paducah toward Columbus got Polk's attention briefly, slowing the flow of reinforcements to Camp Johnston, but in reality did not amount to much, and no Union troops kept Confederate artillery in Columbus from causing Grant problems at Belmont. Smith blamed incompetent subordinates for the failure to distract the Rebels there.[30]

Despite the fact that he had come perilously close to being trapped, Grant thought that he had accomplished what he set out to do, mainly, causing Leonidas Polk to have second thoughts about sending troops from Columbus to meddle in the surrounding countryside, especially in Missouri. Grant also believed that by moving on Belmont, he had kept Polk from sending reinforcements to Thompson, thereby saving Oglesby from possible defeat. In some respects, this was a classic case of putting a positive light on a campaign that had been marked by close calls. Polk was not overly aggressive—Union pressure in Kentucky soon forced him to abandon Columbus—nor was Oglesby ever in great danger. Grant had certainly gotten Polk's attention but, in the process, risked torpedoing his own Civil War career.[31]

A man who became his close friend and ally, William Tecumseh Sherman, observed in later years that Grant never worried over not being able to see what the enemy was doing, preferring instead to focus on what he wanted to do. This perception of Grant was not always true, but it did seem to be an accurate assessment of his action in initiating the Belmont campaign and the cause of many miscalculations. Grant did not seem to think the Confederates would do what they did—that is, send troops above his position to cut him off. If he counted on Walke to keep reinforcements from crossing the river, that plan, too, failed, though Walke had not received specific instructions to provide such support; there is no indication that Grant even considered that possibility. Brooks Simpson has speculated that Grant had disdain for Pillow, dating from the Mexican War, and during the course of the campaign forgot that Polk commanded the enemy, not Pillow. It seems more likely, however, that in planning his hit-and-run assault on Belmont, Grant had not seriously considered possible enemy countermeasures, and this lack of concern could have proved disastrous.[32]

Grant had nonetheless learned and retained lessons to be drawn upon in the future. As Nathaniel Hughes, the historian of the battle at Belmont, has noted, Grant "had done well. He would do better." After Belmont, as the Union high command stepped back to take a look at strategic options, Grant's army remained idle for several weeks. During this time of drill and refitting, Grant found himself working for a new boss, Henry W. Halleck. A brilliant eccentric,

Halleck would hover ominously over Grant's military career for many months to come. Appointed to head the Department of the Missouri by George McClellan, who commanded the U.S. Army at the time, Halleck learned that he was expected to clean up administrative messes and to concentrate as much of his military force as possible along the Mississippi. The instructions he received were not specific, however, only that he must be "prepared for such ulterior operations as the public interests may demand." Halleck changed Grant's command from Southeast Missouri to the District of Cairo, including Smith's position at the mouths of the Tennessee and the Cumberland rivers where they emptied into the Ohio.[33]

As the year 1861 wound down and 1862 dawned, Union strategists, specifically Halleck and McClellan, considered the next Federal moves in the western theater. The Confederate line in Kentucky, intended to block Union penetration into the south, ran from Columbus on the Mississippi eastward to Bowling Green and Mill Springs. The Rebels had troops at these three points and on the banks of the Cumberland and Tennessee rivers, which crossed western Tennessee and Kentucky on their way to the Ohio River. Somewhere along this Rebel line, Federal forces had to make a move, and to the trained military eye, maps of the region suggested that the two rivers might well be used as arrows penetrating the heart of the western Confederacy. U. S. Grant understood those possibilities well enough and wanted to take advantage of them.

NOTES

1. Grant, *Memoirs*, 152–73; Simpson, *Grant*, 87–89; John Y. Simon, ed., *The Personal Memoirs of Julia Dent Grant* (New York, 1975), 89–142.

2. Grant, *Memoirs*, 168, 171–72; Simpson, *Grant*, 89. Jefferson C. Davis was not related to Confederate president Jefferson Davis.)

3. Grant, *Memoirs*, 172.

4. *The War of the Rebellion: A Compilation of the Official Recrods of the Union and Confederate Armies*, 128 vols. (Washington, DC, 1880–1901), ser. 1, vol. 3, p. 470 (hereafter cited as *OR*, followed by series number, volume number, part number where applicable, and page numbers); Grant, *Memoirs*, 172–73.

5. *OR*, ser. 1, vol. 3, pp. 149–50, 476.

6. Ibid., vol. 4, p. 197; Grant, *Memoirs*, 175; Simpson, *Grant*, 92.

7. Grant, *Memoirs*, 176.

8. *OR*, ser. 1, vol. 3, p. 267.

9. Ibid., 268.

10. Ibid., 269.

11. Nathaniel C. Hughes Jr., *The Battle of Belmont: Grant Strikes South* (Chapel Hill, NC, 1991), 55–56.

12. *OR*, ser. 1, vol. 3, pp. 269–70.

13. Hughes, *Belmont*, 57; William B. Feis, *Grant's Secret Service: The Intelligence War from Belmont to Appomattox* (Lincoln, NE, 2002), 45–47; John Y. Simon, ed., *The Papers of U. S. Grant*, 22 vols. to date (Carbondale, IL, 1967–), 3:149–52.

14. *OR*, ser. 1, vol. 3, pp. 269–70.

15. Hughes, *Belmont*, 57.

16. *OR*, ser. 1, vol. 3, pp. 275–76.

17. Ibid., pp. 278–79, 291–94; Simon, *Papers of Grant*, 3:138

18. Simpson, *Grant*, 99.

19. *OR*, ser. 1, vol. 3, p. 279.

20. Ibid., 276.

21. Ibid., 315; Hughes, *Belmont*, 83.

22. *OR*, ser. 1, vol. 3, pp. 270, 280, 308; Grant, *Memoirs*, 182–84.

23. *OR*, ser. 1, vol. 3, pp. 270, 280–81.

24. Grant, *Memoirs*, 180.

25. Roy P. Basler, ed., *The Collected Works of Abraham Lincoln*, 8 vols. plus index (New Brunswick, NJ, 1953–1955), 5:20; Hughes, *Belmont*, 195–96, 202–5.

26. Grant, *Memoirs*, 183, 185; Simon, *Papers of Grant*, 3:137–38.

27. Grant, *Memoirs*, 184.

28. *OR*, ser. 1, vol. 3, pp. 270–71, 281; Hughes, *Belmont*, 175; Grant, *Memoirs*, 184.

29. Hughes, *Belmont*, 184–85.

30. *OR*, ser. 1, vol. 3, pp. 256–57, 272, 299–300; Grant, *Memoirs*, 185; Hughes, *Belmont*, 199–200.

31. Grant, *Memoirs*, 185–86.

32. Simpson, *Grant*, 33, 103; Lloyd Lewis, *Sherman: Fighting Prophet* (New York, 1932), 424.

33. Hughes, *Belmont*, 207; Grant, *Memoirs*, 189; *OR*, ser. 1, vol. 3, p. 568.

CHAPTER THREE

FORTS HENRY AND DONELSON

EARLY IN JANUARY 1862, Ulysses Grant was disappointed to receive, via Henry Halleck, instructions from George McClellan to demonstrate against Columbus, Kentucky, and forts on the Cumberland and Tennessee rivers in order to aid General Don Carlos Buell. Currently, at Louisville, Buell then commanded the Department of the Ohio and faced Confederate forces at Bowling Green, Kentucky, led by Simon Bolivar Buckner. Assuming that his diversion would facilitate Buell's campaign against Buckner, and accepting that he must be a team player even when he did not have the major role, Grant uncomplainingly made plans. Whether intentional strategy or the nature of the man or both, Grant's attitude served him well, for official Washington grew weary of generals who spent most of their time complaining. An officer such as Grant, who quietly did his job as ordered, found favor in the White House and the War Department.[1]

Grant sent C. F. Smith up the west bank of the Tennessee to threaten Fort Heiman, located on high ground across the river from Fort Henry. John McClernand meanwhile marched into western Kentucky and menaced Confederates in Columbus as well as those camped along the Tennessee. Grant traveled with McClernand's division on its diversionary campaign, and the operation made slow progress due to wet, cold weather. Nevertheless, it helped persuade the Confederates not to send reinforcements to Buckner after Rebel forces were defeated by a detachment from George Thomas's division at Mill Springs, Kentucky, on January 19. That Union victory permanently broke the long, tenuous Rebel defensive line across Kentucky and paved the way for further Union operations.

January campaigning also revealed the dominance of the Federal navy on inland rivers. Smith had been able to occupy the mouths of two strategically significant rivers and to operate along the banks of the Tennessee without interference from Confederate vessels. The Rebels had no navy worthy of the name and had to rely on heavy, nonmobile, land batteries to resist Union boats. Smith recognized the advantages and reported to Grant that Fort Heiman, with the assistance of the navy, could be taken.[2]

In his memoirs, Grant claimed to have decided earlier "that the true line of operations for us was up the Tennessee and Cumberland rivers. With us there, the enemy would be compelled to fall back on the east and west entirely out of the State of Kentucky." Before the operations to aid Buell began, Grant had requested but not received permission to travel to St. Louis to discuss this concept with Halleck. Now that Smith had made a similar proposal, Grant asked again and was allowed to go to Halleck's headquarters.[3]

The two men had known each other only slightly in the prewar army, and Halleck did not seem pleased to be bothered by Grant or his plan. Grant later admitted, "I was received with so little cordiality that I perhaps stated the object of my visit with less clearness than I might have done, and I had not uttered many sentences before I was cut short as if my plan was preposterous." Dejected, Grant traveled back to Cairo. Perhaps his seemingly permanent rumpled appearance had put off the fastidious Halleck. Or perhaps Halleck, who had a quick military mind and already knew that Grant's proposal was the correct strategy to follow, felt offended that one of his officers would travel to his headquarters and point out the obvious.[4]

Whatever the case, the meeting set an unfortunate precedent for future relations between the two generals. Each had ambitions, and each was anxious to make a name in this war. Halleck cared little for underlings; he sought the approval of the powerful in the White House and the War Department. Grant saw fighting the war in the field as his ticket to whatever measure of fame he might achieve. He detested the politics of command, preferring to absorb necessary techniques and develop skills that would serve him well. He and Halleck would never be close friends, and Grant seemed slow at first to understand that if he stumbled, Halleck could do him harm. As time passed, they learned to tolerate and even respect each other—Grant occasionally bragged about Halleck's ability—but the development of mutual trust took them down a long, tortuous road. They would succeed or fail in spite of their relationship, not because of it.

Grant seemed to give himself too much credit for the rivers concept in his postwar writings. In correspondence much closer to the actual events, he noted that the Union navy's reconnaissance

U. S. Grant, 1862. From the author's collection.

up the Tennessee and Cumberland during preceding months had
made the campaign an obvious next step, and "it accomplished little
to credit any particular general with first proposing the idea." No
doubt the plan evolved from staff discussions and officers talking
among themselves. Maps clearly indicating the Union opportunities presented by the rivers were easily understood by soldiers with
even limited formal military training. The Cumberland and Tennessee provided channels of penetration into the western Confederate heartland, and the South, without a significant navy, had to

depend on forts occupied by infantry and armed with heavy artillery to defend against combined army and navy Federal operations.

Much to his delight, Grant soon found a significant ally to support the proposed two-river campaign. He and veteran navy commander Andrew Foote, a flag officer in charge of vessels stationed at Cairo, discussed strategy, and Foote heartily approved ascending the Tennessee. Encouraged, Grant renewed his written requests to Halleck for proceeding with the campaign, and Foote sent along a written endorsement. On February 1, Grant received Halleck's permission to attack the Tennessee River forts.[5]

Grant had boats on hand at Cairo, because the closure of Mississippi River commerce to the south had idled many vessels and river men. Yet the movement of some 17,000 men up the Ohio to Paducah would require even more boats and crews, so Grant ordered only about half his force, commanded by McClernand, to board the available transports. McClernand proceeded up the Ohio and into the Tennessee to a point some 9 miles from Fort Henry. Grant soon arrived and sent transports back downriver to Paducah to pick up C. F. Smith's division.

Before sending the boats back, however, Grant led a reconnaissance upstream to see whether his troops could land south of a small creek, flooded by recent rains, that cut inland to the east above Fort Henry. From aboard the *Essex* he watched for signs of Confederate resistance as the gunboat steamed past the creek mouth toward Henry. Rebel artillery fired at the intruders, but shells initially fell short; only when a long-range rifled piece opened fire did a shell penetrate the deck. Grant had seen enough to believe that his army could land uncontested south of the creek.[6] Soon Union troops streamed ashore, and as quickly as transports emptied, they went back to Paducah to pick up Smith's men. The operation went more slowly than the impatient Grant anticipated, and at last he issued orders for an advance upon Fort Henry at 11:00 A.M. on February 6. He felt confident that all his troops would be on hand by then and ready to go.

Grant intended to approach along the east bank at a bend in the Tennessee. Fewer than 3,000 Confederates occupied extensive works from that point toward Fort Donelson, which lay on the west bank of the Cumberland some 10 miles east of Fort Henry. High water due to overflowing creeks made it difficult for the Rebel defenders at the two forts to support each other in case of attack. Directly across the Tennessee lay Fort Heiman on higher ground, manned but unfinished and not yet armed with cannon. Grant feared that if he did not move quickly, the Confederates would send reinforcements to the area and present an obstacle that he could not overcome. "Prompt action on our part," he later recalled, "was imperative." He never wanted to give the enemy time to seize the initiative.[7]

Charles F. Smith. From Ezra J. Warner, *Generals in Blue: Lives of the Union Commanders* (Baton Rouge: Louisiana State University Press, 1964), 455.

His plan of attack was simple. Foote's gunboats and Grant's army would attack as simultaneously as conditions allowed. The army would pin the Confederates in their trenches while navy guns pounded the seventeen pieces of Rebel field artillery. Smith's division would land on the west side of the river and assault Fort

Heiman from the rear. High water, dense woods, and few passable roads slowed McClernand's infantry on the east side of the Tennessee, but, as it turned out, none of that mattered.[8]

Lloyd Tilghman, commanding Confederate forces at Fort Henry, realized he could be trapped and ordered an evacuation, except for an artillery detachment that stayed behind to delay the Yankees. He had earlier abandoned Heiman, leaving only a few cavalry to harass Smith's approaching columns, and now most of his troops fled to Fort Donelson, except for Tilghman himself and about ninety men, who, along with the artillery and supplies, fell into the hands of Grant's forces. The only Union casualties of note took place aboard the *Essex* when an enemy shell exploded the boiler, killing or wounding some forty-eight men.[9]

Grant proudly reported to Halleck his success at Fort Henry and asserted that on February 8 he would finish the job by taking Fort Donelson. He should not have made so bold a prediction at a time of year when weather, however unpredictable, was predictably bad; heavy rains turned already wet roads into quagmires. Grant realized, too, that there would be a necessary delay to give the navy time to go downstream to Paducah in order to ascend the Cumberland. While he waited for better weather and for the navy to get into position, Grant, his staff, and a cavalry detachment scouted the outer works west of Donelson.[10]

Throughout the war, Grant demonstrated his skill, honed at West Point, of evaluating others, especially Rebel commanders opposing him. He felt confident that General Gideon Pillow, with whom he had served in Mexico and who had always had more mouth than nerve, would not offer stiff opposition. As for Pillow's fellow officers, John Floyd, commanding at Donelson, "was no soldier," and Buckner, though capable, was too far down the chain of command to have an impact on strategy and tactics. Grant's surmises proved correct in this instance, though he showed the same tendency he had demonstrated at Belmont to underestimate enemy options.[11]

The scouting trip revealed that two roads led to the Donelson area, one directly to the fort and the other to the town of Dover, about two river miles to the south. Reports indicated that on the east, Donelson fronted the Cumberland; north of the fort flowed swollen Hickman Creek, and to the south a partly flooded ravine and Indian Creek ran west to east into the river. Strategically placed rifle pits and big guns made Donelson a much more formidable obstacle than Henry. Broken terrain blocked with abatis meant that it would be difficult to reduce the fort with an infantry assault.

While Grant pondered the situation, he grew concerned that Halleck remained quiet on the subject of the campaign; he did not know that a Rebel telegrapher had intercepted his messages to St. Louis and that therefore his superior had not heard from him. He learned much later that his perceived silence had infuriated both Halleck and George McClellan. The snafu did not interrupt the campaign, but Halleck's anger took some time to subside. Grant did receive word that Halleck wanted Federal troops to dig in at Fort Henry, but by the time that message arrived, he was already closing on the outer enemy works at Donelson. As he demonstrated time and again, and to him it was only common sense, Grant had no intention of obeying superfluous orders when the next victory seemed close at hand.[12]

In his memoirs, Grant recalled his anxiety as he rushed to overthrow Donelson: "I was very impatient, . . . because I knew the importance of the place to the enemy and supposed he would reinforce it rapidly." He talked with Foote, and soon gunboats ascended the Cumberland to join in the attack. Welcome reinforcements arrived at Henry on transports; Grant ordered a brigade led by John Thayer to stay aboard and go under the protection of Foote's gunboats back to the Ohio and up the Cumberland. Grant had learned from the Belmont experience that having friendly troops on his left flank greatly enhanced his gunboat cover.[13]

Meanwhile, Union troops marched east from Henry, some 15,000 of Smith's and McClernand's men, plus eight batteries and a cavalry regiment. Smith left behind part of a division, commanded by Lew Wallace, to watch the Henry and Heiman areas in case the Confederates tried to get behind Federal lines. As the Union forces advanced, Smith's division occupied the left and McClernand's the right. The same hilly terrain that protected the Confederates defending Donelson shielded Grant's men as they advanced. As the weather improved, troops still too green in army life to know better tossed their blankets away. Soon winter blasts permeated central Tennessee with frigid air and frozen precipitation, and many Federals, often forced to camp without the benefit of fires for the sake of security, experienced "much discomfort and absolute suffering."[14]

February 12 and 13 passed quietly as Grant waited for Foote to get into position, along with Thayer's infantry, and Wallace arrived from Fort Henry to command the center of the Union line. The only excitement of note came on the thirteenth when McClernand, neglecting to check with Grant, sent several regiments to assault a Rebel battery that had been pounding the Federal right. The battery had ample infantry support, and McClernand's sortie accomplished little other than to subject his troops to heavy enemy fire. Grant preferred aggressive subordinates, but when they acted too rashly—and especially if the name of the general in question was McClernand—he had reason to be irritated. Growing casualty lists forced Union surgeons to search the sparsely settled region for houses to convert into hospitals. Despite McClernand's foray and the logistical challenges of setting up hospitals, Grant's lines continued to converge on Confederate defenses, thanks in part to the Union naval shells that helped to buffer Rebel resistance. Grant's appreciation of the navy continued to grow.[15]

Foote finally arrived on the evening of the thirteenth with his flotilla, which included three of the new ironclads—the *St. Louis*, the *Louisville*, and the *Pittsburg*—and two wooden gunboats serving as transports for Thayer's brigade. Rather than leave Thayer on the far left, Grant sent these troops to Wallace in the center, where with other reinforcements they formed a new division commanded by Wallace. The extra manpower also allowed Smith and McClernand to strengthen their lines on the left and right, respectively. With his line anchored on the Cumberland above and below Donelson, with gunboats controlling the river north to the Ohio, and with no additional Confederate forces of any size on the horizon, Grant felt secure. He did not expect a repetition of the unexpected enemy troop movements that had caused him trouble at Belmont.

At this point, Grant's overall plan to force the surrender of Donelson included siege tactics, which would hold the Confederates where they were while Foote's gunboats attempted to batter the fort's big guns into submission. He hoped that some of the boats could run past Donelson to Dover. With both gunboats and troops on McClernand's far right in that sector, Grant should be able to cut off Donelson's defenders completely from reinforcements or logistical succor.

On the afternoon of the fourteenth, Foote's boats steamed upriver toward Donelson, and the advance boat reached within 200 yards of the fort before concentrated Confederate fire inflicted serious damage on the flotilla. The Union vessels retreated, ending a

BATTLE OF FORT DONELSON
February 13–16, 1862

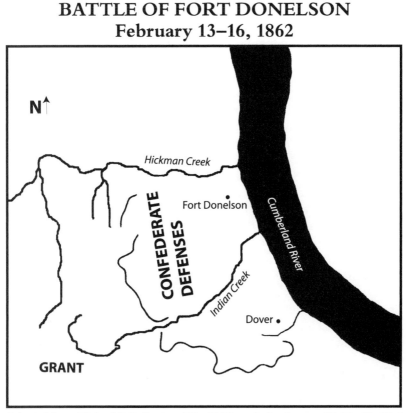

Adapted from Michael B. Ballard and David Muench, *Landscapes of Battle: The Civil War* (Jackson: University Press of Mississippi, 1988), 17.

thunderous artillery duel. Jubilant Rebels cheered and sent messages to Richmond telling of a great victory on the Cumberland. A disappointed Grant stretched out on his cot that night "not knowing but that I would have to intrench my position, and bring up tents for the men or build huts under the cover of the hills."[16]

The next morning he arose to find a message from Foote asking Grant to meet him on board the flagship; he had been hurt during the previous day's fight and did not think he could continue in command. Preparing to leave for the meeting, Grant instructed his staff to spread the word to field commanders to do "nothing to bring on an engagement until they received further orders, but to hold their positions." Grant rode over rugged terrain, made worse by the many muddy ruts now frozen solid, to the Cumberland above Donelson, where a small boat carried him out to Foote.[17]

Foote asked for time; he assured Grant that both he and his damaged boats could be ready for action within ten days. Grant decided that he must therefore commence full siege operations until the navy could right itself. He no doubt believed the Confederates could and would do nothing, especially with Floyd and other incompetents making decisions.[18] There were legitimate reasons to believe the Rebels would not attack: Grant now had more troops than when the campaign started, and, despite the repulse of the navy, Union vessels still controlled the river. Unexpected circumstances, however, once more interfered. On the night of February 14, Floyd, encouraged by the work of the Donelson batteries and by the opinions of his officers, decided to attack Grant's lines at daylight on the fifteenth in an effort, he said, "to cut open a route of exit for our troops to the interior of the country, and thus save our army." Pillow, supported and followed by Buckner, would make the assault on McClernand's position. Once roadways to the south had been cleared, the Confederates could escape.[19]

When the Rebel attack began early on the fifteenth, the Union line fell back under the pressure of the concentrated Rebel push, though Wallace had the initiative to send reinforcements to help McClernand shore up his battered division. It was the Confederates themselves who negated their advantages. Poor tactical decisions, such as not holding back reserves to continue pressuring the Union line, and lack of coordination doomed the assault. As historian Benjamin Cooling has noted, "Each of the Confederate generals seemed to be fighting his own isolated battle, only marginally coordinated with the others." With much arguing and poor battlefield leadership, Floyd and his subordinates, Pillow and Buckner, frittered away the opportunity to escape, and the close of the day found surviving Confederate forces back where they had started.[20]

Hearing the commotion, Grant raced to assess the damage, but by the time he arrived, the danger had passed. He observed that McClernand's men had fought well under the circumstances and might have done even better had Federal commanders been more experienced in keeping ammunition supplies conveniently at hand. Somewhat embarrassed that he had once more been caught by surprise, Grant conferred with his staff and concluded that the enemy must surely be demoralized by their failure of the day and vulnerable to a counterattack. He therefore decided to send his rested troops into action against the Confederate right. Riding with his staff to Smith's headquarters, he ordered Smith to send forward his whole division. Smith moved quickly, and by nightfall of February 15 his infantry had captured significant portions of outer enemy works, including high ground that facilitated fire into the interior of Donelson.[21]

Meanwhile, erratic Confederate leadership continued. Floyd, who had been secretary of war under Lincoln's predecessor, James Buchanan, and feared that if captured he might be executed, turned command over to Pillow, who passed the torch to Buckner. Some 3,000 Confederate troops joined Floyd and Pillow in a night flight across the Cumberland, and others followed cavalry commander Nathan Bedford Forrest and his riders in an escape to the south. On February 16, Buckner sent Grant a note requesting terms for the capitulation of Fort Donelson.[22] Grant responded with words that propelled him from a scruffy, ambitious western theater general to a commander of national reputation: "No terms except an unconditional and immediate surrender can be accepted. I propose to move immediately upon your works." His initials provided a convenient method for newspaper reporters to enhance their stories, and Grant became known as "Unconditional Surrender" Grant. Buckner did not contest what he called Grant's "unchivalrous" conditions.[23]

During these latter stages of the campaign, another situation developed that would prove meaningful to Grant's career in a positive way: a fellow Ohioan named William T. Sherman had been ordered to the mouth of the Cumberland to make sure that men and supplies flowed upriver to Grant. Sherman, a prolific letter writer, sent numerous encouraging messages by boat to Grant, a particularly gratifying gesture since at the time he outranked Grant. As the years passed, the two came to share disappointments and triumphs and built a close, enduring friendship. For Grant, just knowing Sherman was around and always ready to stand by him was a source of immeasurable comfort and assurance as he faced future challenges of expanded responsibilities.[24]

After Fort Donelson, at a time when he should have been reaping rewards from his triumph, Grant received a slight from Halleck, a portent of things to come. Halleck nominated Grant, Buell, and Pope for promotion to major general, and suggested to Washington that he, Halleck, be made overall commander in the West. Since he was still unhappy with Grant's loose command style, Halleck may have sent three names to downplay the importance of Grant's victory on the Cumberland. Or perhaps he wanted official

Washington to appreciate his whole team of western commanders, rather than focusing on just one. Whatever his reasons, Lincoln refused to go along and forwarded only Grant's nomination to Congress for approval.[25]

Henry Halleck. From Ezra J. Warner, *Generals in Blue: Lives of the Union Commanders* (Baton Rouge: Louisiana State University Press, 1964), 195.

More trouble then erupted between Grant and Halleck. By his very nature, Grant wanted to stay on the offensive. Maps revealed that a steady push south, led by one overall coordinating commander, would enhance the capture of Henry and Donelson. Hence, Grant sent word to Halleck that the way to Clarksville and Nashville, Tennessee, lay open; unless he received orders to the contrary, he intended to push on and take both. Such presumption indicated Grant's high confidence level and demonstrated again that he did not want his momentum slowed by delayed orders. Receiving no response by February 21, he sent Smith to Clarksville—which by then the Confederates had deserted—and reinforcements to assist Don Carlos Buell, who, Grant learned, was advancing on Nashville. Still hearing no objections from Halleck, he traveled to Nashville himself and found Buell intent on concentrating Union forces north of the Cumberland to meet a nonexistent enemy threat.[26]

As mentioned earlier, the lack of response from headquarters it was due to persistent interference with Union communications at Cairo, where an undercover Rebel telegrapher was creating disruptions. The only message that did get through from Halleck, dated March 1, ordered Grant to leave a small force to secure Donelson and to take the rest of his army back to Fort Henry; a major move up the Tennessee to Eastport, Mississippi, had been planned, and Grant's force was to join the expedition. That made sense, but then, on March 4, Grant received a bombshell from Halleck: "You will place Maj.-Gen. C. F. Smith in command of expedition, and remain yourself at Fort Henry. Why do you not obey my orders to report strength and positions of your command?"[27]

Dumbfounded, Grant learned for the first time that he was required to make such reports. He should have considered possible reasons for Halleck's silence, especially in a region where the populace had very mixed views about the war. And he certainly should have been less presumptuous after the strained meeting in St. Louis. Adopting the tenuous position that as long as he received no orders to the contrary he could proceed as he wished made him vulnerable to criticism from his superiors. Now, Halleck added that he had been "advised to arrest" Grant for going to Nashville without authority. Infuriated by the tone of the message, Grant "turned over the command as directed and then replied to General Halleck courteously, but asked to be relieved from further duty under him."[28]

He soon learned that Halleck's anger resulted from the latter's inability to answer a request by McClellan for details about his overall troop strength. Halleck had been requesting more reinforcements, but before he sent them, McClellan wanted to know how many men Halleck already had in the field, and in order to compile that figure, Halleck had requested troop strength information from his commanders. He exaggerated the number of such inquiries he had sent but, having no other explanation for Grant's silence, Halleck assumed that he was being insubordinate and complained to Washington—throwing in for good measure Grant's unauthorized move to Nashville. On the basis of Halleck's complaint, McClellan ordered him to relieve Grant from duty, investigate his actions, and arrest him. On March 13, Grant again asked Halleck to relieve him "until I can be placed right in the estimation of those higher in authority."[29]

The irony of being treated in such a manner on the heels of his victories at Henry and Donelson did not escape Grant and no doubt fueled his anger, but his nightmare turned out to be brief. On March 13 he heard that he had been restored to command. Halleck, as he was wont to do in uncomfortable circumstances, did not admit his own role in instigating the charges against Grant but said that he had responded to charges initiated in Washington and, in the process, had completely exonerated Grant. Rather than admit that his own fury had led to McClellan's actions, Halleck wrote Grant, "Instead of relieving you, I wish you, as soon as your new army is in the field, to assume immediate command, and lead it to new victories." Grant did not learn the whole truth of this affair until several years later. Yet he was not guiltless, for maintaining contact with his superiors was as much his responsibility as theirs, but he continued to believe that unless reined in, he could carry out his campaign plans unimpeded. Ironically, Halleck eventually adopted a pattern of behavior that allowed, and even encouraged, his subordinates to carry out their operations without interference from him.[30]

Grant must have been encouraged by the impressive list of people who defended him during the controversy: Congressman Elihu Washburne; many of Grant's own subordinates, including John McClernand; and Charles Dana, at the time a reporter and, more important, a confidant of Secretary of War Edwin Stanton. Soon the situation boomeranged on Halleck, who received a pointed message from Washington: "It has been reported, that soon after the battle of Fort Donelson, Brigadier-General Grant left his command without leave. By direction of the President, the Secretary of War desires you to ascertain and report whether General Grant left his command at any time without proper authority, and, if so, for how long; whether he has made to you proper reports and returns of his force; whether he has committed any acts which are unauthorized or not in accordance with military subordination or propriety, and, if so, what." About the same time, Halleck received what he had longed for, command of all Union armies in the western theater. Satisfied, he decided to retreat from his campaign against Grant, for it was clear that Lincoln had suspicions about the validity of the charges, and Halleck knew that he had no proof with which to convict Grant on any of them.[31]

Though restored to command, Grant had been a victim not only of partisan infiltration of Federal telegraphy operations but also of jealousy and loose talk, for Halleck wanted to take credit for the successful Henry-Donelson campaign and seemed willing to smear Grant to get him out of the way. Halleck also assumed the worst about Grant when requested paperwork did not arrive. Certainly he resented Grant's notoriety and, after fuming for a while, had sent accusatory messages to Washington. His bitterness and pettiness were apparent in a portion of a March 3 message to McClellan: "Satisfied with his victory, he [Grant] sits down and enjoys it without any regard to the future. I am worn-out and tired with this neglect and inefficiency." Halleck also implied that Grant might have been drinking; the old army gossip had come back to haunt the general, and not for the last time.[32]

Clearly, Halleck had slanted the truth. Soon he backed off, not of his own volition, but because he could not back up his charges and because George McClellan was removed as general in chief of the Union forces. Halleck now had no ally, and having exaggerated the accusations against Grant, he at once recanted, called the situation a "misunderstanding," and informed Grant of his reinstatement. Grant had some Washington connections, especially Washburne, politically powerful and a friend of Lincoln, and Halleck did not want to overplay a weak hand; he had, after all, received overall command in the West. The strained relationship between Grant and Halleck, in part the fault of both men, continued to plague Grant's career in the western theater, especially in his next campaign.[33]

Before that campaign picked up momentum, however, Grant had to deal with administrative matters that, though troubling, gave him valuable experience. He reorganized his staff in an effort to tighten the reins on his army's activities between battles. He tried to solve such problems as pillaging and theft, the misuse of freed black labor, and malicious reporting by unfriendly newspaper correspondents. (He shared his distrust of reporters with his new friend

Sherman, who fared even worse among newsmen.) Grant also had to fight off physical maladies, especially chills, fevers, and stomach problems, as well as contend with family feuding back home in Illinois, where Julia was having trouble getting along with her sisters-in-law.

Despite the controversy with Halleck, Grant had become a hero in the Union, a man who had won a campaign and whose future had survived a threat and seemed promising. His soldiers believed in him now more than ever, for he had led them to victory and acclaim. Like their leader, they were maturing as they faced the trials of campaigning. They understood clearly that soldiering was not a nonstop charge to glory but serious work, with death looming very close. Grant and his army were bonding in ways that only they could understand and appreciate.

Grant's insistence on unconditional surrender at Donelson had indeed played well in the press, in Washington, and across the North. Whether intentionally or not, he had taken advantage of a hunger in Union states for good news from the front by making a forceful statement to a Rebel general. The simple, strong wording, typical of Grant's approach to life in general and command in particular, resonated with the public, and if he did not plan it so, he certainly understood the results. He was learning, sometimes the hard way, that a general in charge of a campaign did not, indeed could not, operate in a vacuum. Even in the West, he could not escape the spotlight that came with command responsibilities.

During the campaign, Grant had once more shown aggressive tendencies: he had seized the initiative and held it. Regardless of weak enemy leadership, his performance had been solid. The surprise attack on his right had, if anything, made him more determined to finish off the enemy. Overall, he had handled his troops well, maintained the cooperation of the navy, and shown an understanding of war lacking in many Federal generals. The way to win was to go hard after the enemy and keep up the pressure.

Although the controversy with Halleck had caught Grant by surprise, he had not panicked, and his strong showing thus far in the war, plus an array of supporters, had helped him survive. The peaks and valleys of generalship would continue to test him; when he rejoined his army in Savannah, Tennessee, he did not know that another valley—a deep one—lay just ahead. His tendency to underestimate and misread the enemy would cause him more anxious moments, and his nemesis Halleck would be waiting to pounce.[34]

NOTES

1. Grant, *Memoirs*, 189; Simon, *Papers of Grant*, 4:3–4.
2. Grant, *Memoirs*, 189; Simon, *Papers of Grant*, 4:10–11.
3. Grant, *Memoirs*, 189.
4. Ibid., 190.
5. Benjamin F. Cooling, *Forts Henry and Donelson: The Key to the Confederate Heartland* (Knoxville, TN, 1987), 65–66; *OR*, ser. 1, vol. 7, pp. 120–22; McFeely, *Grant*, 120.
6. Grant, *Memoirs*, 190.
7. Ibid., 192; *OR*, ser. 1, vol. 7, pp. 124–26, 581.
8. Grant, *Memoirs*, 192; Simon, *Papers of Grant*, 4:150–51.
9. Grant, *Memoirs*, 192; *OR*, ser. 1, vol. 7, p. 125.
10. *OR*, ser. 1, vol. 7, p. 124; Grant, *Memoirs*, 196.
11. Grant, *Memoirs*, 196.
12. Ibid., 196–97; *OR*, ser. 1, vol. 7, pp. 595, 600.
13. Grant, *Memoirs*, 197–98; Simon, *Papers of Grant*, 4:182.
14. Grant, *Memoirs*, 198; Simon, *Papers of Grant*, 4:207.
15. Grant, *Memoirs*, 198, 201; *OR*, ser. 1, vol. 7, p. 159.
16. Grant, *Memoirs*, 201–3; *OR*, ser. 1, vol. 7, p. 159.
17. Grant, *Memoirs*, 203; Simon, *Papers of Grant*, 4:216.
18. Grant, *Memoirs*, 203; *OR*, ser. 1, vol. 7, p. 159.
19. Grant, *Memoirs*, 203; *OR*, ser. 1, vol. 7, pp. 281–82.
20. Cooling, *Forts*, 172, 174; *OR*, ser. 1, vol. 7, p. 159.
21. *OR*, ser. 1, vol. 7, pp. 159–60; Simon, *Papers of Grant*, 4:216; Cooling, *Forts*, 172, 174.
22. *OR*, ser. 1, vol. 7, p. 160; Grant, *Memoirs*, 207.
23. *OR*, ser. 1, vol. 7, p. 161.
24. Ibid., p. 638; Grant, *Memoirs*, 213.
25. McFeely, *Grant*, 104; *OR*, ser. 1, vol. 7, p. 628.
26. Grant, *Memoirs*, 215–16.
27. Ibid., 220; *OR*, ser. 1, vol. 7, p. 674; Simon, *Papers of Grant*, 4:319.
28. Grant, *Memoirs*, 220.
29. Ibid.; Simon, *Papers of Grant*, 4:320, 331, 334–35.
30. Grant, *Memoirs*, 221; Simon, *Papers of Grant*, 4:354–55.
31. Adam Badeau, *Military History of Ulysses S. Grant, from April, 1861 to April, 1865*, 2 vols. (New York, 1868), 1:63; Simpson, *Grant*, 124.
32. *OR*, ser. 1, vol. 7, p. 680; McFeely, *Grant*, 109.
33. Simpson, *Grant*, 120–25.
34. Ibid., 125–27; Cooling, *Forts*, 213, 245, 252.

CHAPTER FOUR

SHILOH

IN LATER YEARS, U. S. Grant recalled the situation he found upon returning to his troops:

> When I reassumed command on the 17th of March I found the army divided, about half being on the east bank of the Tennessee at Savannah, while one division was at Crump's landing on the west bank about four miles higher up, and the remainder at Pittsburg landing, five miles above Crump's [Landing]. The enemy was in force at Corinth [Mississippi], the junction of the two most important railroads in the Mississippi valley—one connecting Memphis and the Mississippi River with the East, and the other leading south to all the cotton states. Still another railroad connects Corinth with Jackson, in west Tennessee.

Grant knew if he took Corinth, he would cripple Confederate logistics and facilitate future operations against Vicksburg.[1]

Grant was writing with the benefit of hindsight, of course, but his summary is a succinct review of the situation in March 1862 and the high stakes of a potential confrontation with Confederate general Albert Sidney Johnston. Grant's account in his memoirs of the Shiloh campaign is especially important, since he never wrote a detailed, official report.

The campaign began with the Union seemingly having the upper hand. After abandoning Nashville, Sidney Johnston had retreated southeast down the railroad leading to Chattanooga. The rest of his force, commanded by P. G. T. Beauregard, was farther west, scattered along the Mississippi River. The way stood open for Grant's Army of the Tennessee, with the support of Don Carlos Buell's Army of the Ohio, to push south between the divided Confederate forces and attack either one, or both. Yet taking advantage of Johnston and Beauregard would require Grant and Buell to cooperate and coordinate their movements over rugged terrain and bad roads—and without the benefit of railroads, for the available rail lines, running east and west, favored Confederate movements. Rather than rush into an offensive, then, Union generals worked to coordinate their advance, with Buell marching southwest from Nashville to join Grant in the Savannah-Pittsburg Landing-Crump's Landing area of Tennessee, some 25 miles or so north by northeast of Corinth, Mississippi.

Using railroads to concentrate, Johnston and Beauregard joined forces, an aggregate of some 40,300 men, at Corinth two weeks before Buell got close to Grant's position. An earlier attempt by William T. Sherman to cut the Rebel rail line running east from Corinth had been doomed by high backwater from the Tennessee. The Confederates hoped to have more men soon, especially Earl Van Dorn's army in Arkansas, which was hurrying toward the Mississippi in an effort to participate with Johnston's planned move against Grant. Grant had some 42,600 men, but Buell's 20,000 would give him a considerable advantage. Johnston and Beauregard knew that Buell was en route to join Grant and thus hastened to attack Grant's concentration of forces camped on high ground near Pittsburg Landing before Buell could get there.[2]

On March 17, Grant had five divisions on the banks of the Tennessee: C. F. Smith's (General W. H. L. Wallace temporarily in command because of Smith's illness, which proved to be fatal), McClernand's, Sherman's, Lew Wallace's, and Stephen Hurlbut's. Unattached reinforcements formed a new division commanded by Benjamin Prentiss. Grant expected to take the offensive as soon as Buell arrived. His boss, Henry Halleck, cautioned against aggression until reinforcements were at hand. "We must strike no blow," he warned Grant, "until we are strong enough to admit no doubt of the result." Grant, however, wrote Halleck on March 21: "The temper of the Rebel troops is such that there is but little doubt that Corinth will fall much more easily than Donelson did when we do move." He believed the enemy troops to be tired and vulnerable.[3]

Grant saw no need for his army to dig in. Convinced that the Rebels would not take the offensive, an optimistic, enthusiastic Grant dismissed the idea of fortifications of any kind. James McPherson, one of his subordinates and a skilled engineer, examined the area for possible entrenchments and reported to Grant that the army would have to pull back closer to the Tennessee in order to take advantage of the terrain. Such a line would present logistical problems and gave Grant a further excuse to dismiss the idea of digging ditches. Early in the war, neither generals nor armies thought much about using shovels and dirt for protection, though experience would teach them the benefits of earthworks.

As Grant later admitted, "The fact is, I regarded the campaign we were engaged in as an offensive one and had no idea that the enemy would leave strong intrenchments to take the initiative when he knew he would be attacked where he was if he remained." Yet "every precaution" was taken, Grant insisted, "and every effort made to keep advised of all movements of the enemy." The precautions and efforts proved grossly inadequate. Emboldened by his victories at Henry and Donelson and perhaps feeling encouraged by his reinstatement, Grant was eager to demonstrate how wrong Halleck had been to embarrass him, and once again his notions of the enemy's strategic thinking were much in error. He wanted so desperately to refurbish his tarnished "unconditional surrender" image that he became careless. Shiloh historian Larry Daniel has noted: "The fact is, Grant simply did not anticipate that the enemy would be so audacious as to leave a fortified base. Underestimation of the enemy, neglect, fear of losing the aggressive touch, failure to learn from his Fort Donelson experience—all played a role in this grave blunder."[4]

On April 1, Johnston began moving his army toward Pittsburg Landing. Cavalry skirmishing characterized the advance, and Union officers saw little reason for alarm. Grant later admitted having some anxiety, based on the reported disposition of enemy troops, that Crump's Landing might be their target, but he was confident that both Pittsburg and Crump could be defended.[5]

While waiting for Buell, Grant had periodically visited the encampment at Pittsburg Landing, returning to his headquarters in Savannah each evening. He claimed that he would have preferred moving to Pittsburg, but assuming that Buell would first arrive at Savannah, he wanted to be on hand to greet him and plan the coming offensive. The increased skirmishing marking Johnston's march toward Grant's army, however, caused him to delay more and more frequently his nightly return to Savannah. Signs of coming trouble became increasingly obvious, yet Grant adamantly refused to accept the possibility of a major Confederate attack.[6]

On Friday night, April 4, Grant the skilled horseman experienced the embarrassment of having his horse fall. He hurried toward the sound of skirmishing to the south. He wanted to get a firsthand look at the front, but he picked a bad evening to do so: "The night was one of impenetrable darkness, with rain pouring down in torrents; nothing was visible to the eye except as revealed by the frequent flashes of lightning." En route, he ran into W. H. L.

Wallace and McPherson, both of whom assured him that all was now quiet. As he rode back toward Pittsburg, his horse slipped in the mud, and the animal fell, trapping one of Grant's legs beneath the beast's weight. The soft ground helped the general avoid more serious injury, but even so, his bruised and sprained ankle kept him on crutches for several days. Predictably, the nature of the accident fueled rumors of Grant's insobriety, especially after the results of the approaching conflict at Shiloh. Critics seemed to rush to judgment at the slightest hint that Grant's behavior might be the result of inebriation.[7]

At last, on April 5, Buell's advance division marched into Savannah and, following Grant's prior instructions, moved down the east bank of the Tennessee. Grant thought Buell's troops could be quickly ferried across to Pittsburg or to Crump's as needed, since the Confederates posed no naval threat on the Tennessee. When he received word that Buell would be arriving the next day, Grant decided to meet him early and then go down to Pittsburg to check on developments there. He did not know that his information was false, that Buell was already in Savannah, having come the evening of April 5. Grant was still eating breakfast when he heard sounds of heavy firing to the south at Pittsburg.[8]

He wrote a quick flurry of orders, including a note to Buell explaining why he could not meet with him until he found out what was going on. While en route via the Tennessee to Pittsburg Landing, Grant contacted Lew Wallace at Crump's Landing and instructed him to have his men ready to move quickly as circumstances dictated; he still thought Crump's might be the Confederate target. Once he got closer to Pittsburg and confirmed that a major Confederate offensive had rolled into his army there, Grant quickly sent word to Wallace to hurry to Pittsburg. But confusion soon ensued: Wallace marched away from Pittsburg Landing because, he insisted later, the instructions delivered to him were to come up on the Union right. Grant, however, maintained that the order told Wallace only to get to Pittsburg Landing, where the division could be used as needed. No written document survived to settle the matter. The end result was that Wallace marched himself out of the fighting that raged all day on April 6, the first day of the bloody Battle of Shiloh.[9] Grant later gave Wallace the benefit of the doubt, thinking that Wallace had likely believed he could flank the Rebel position and thereby strike a telling blow. In truth, Johnston's attack simply caused chaos, and Grant was unable to put together a timely response. For most of April 6 the army was on its heels, trying desperately to avoid a major defeat, while Wallace marched far on the Union right, unable to find the battlefield where he was desperately needed.[10]

As the fighting developed, Sherman held the Union right, positioned on a ridge between two creeks. The one landmark was an old Methodist meeting house called Shiloh. McClernand occupied the ground to Sherman's left, and Benjamin Prentiss's division camped on McClernand's left. Of these three divisions, only McClernand's had seen much action, having fought at Belmont and in the Henry-Donelson campaign. C. F. Smith's division, commanded by W. H. L. Wallace because of Smith's illness, was in reserve on the right, and David Stuart commanded one of Sherman's brigades on the far left.[11]

Grant busied himself checking logistical matters, including moving wagonloads of ordnance to the front from the landing. In the midst of the fighting, he rode to confer with Sherman, McClernand, and his other generals. Despite the chaotic conditions, he seemed cool and calm. With bullets and artillery shells filling the air, prudent officers tried to stay out of harm's way, but Grant's visits to commanders along the battle lines demonstrated clearly that his battlefield bravery in Mexico had been no aberration. Certainly he understood the danger the army was in, but there is no evidence that he ever panicked. On the contrary, he seemed oblivious to the possibility of being hit.[12]

The Union battle line ran right to left between the two creeks. Johnston intended to drive Grant's left away from the Tennessee, roll up the Federal line on Sherman's position, and push the Federal troops north, away from Pittsburg Landing and out of reach of Union naval support. The Confederate attack came straight at the Union line, however, and Johnston's strategy failed: the Rebel assaults pushed the Federal army straight back toward the Tennessee and the Landing, within easy range of Union naval guns. Johnston fell mortally wounded during the tactical confusion.[13]

At first everything went the Confederates' way, though lack of experience on both sides produced fractured alignments. Johnston's troops often stopped to pick up food and whatever belongings that caught their fancy in camps abandoned by fleeing Union soldiers. Sherman and McClernand managed to avoid being flanked, but as the fighting developed, both were driven back toward Pittsburg Landing. Grant ordered Prentiss to stay put "at all hazards," and

BATTLE OF SHILOH
April 6, 1862

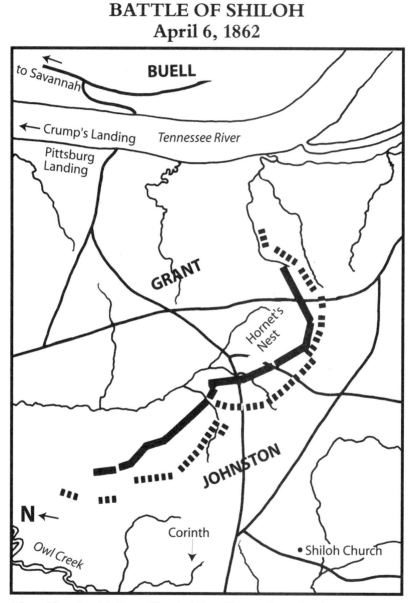

Adapted from Patricia Faust, *Historical Times Illustrated Encyclopedia of the Civil War* (New York: Harper & Row, 1986), 684.

Prentiss managed to fend off assaulting Rebels for some time. Fighting became so fierce that the area came to be called the Hornet's Nest because of the seemingly endless humming of bullets. Eventually, however, Prentiss was cut off and forced to surrender troops of both his and W. H. L. Wallace's divisions.[14] Writing of the fighting long afterward, Grant noted, "It was a case of Southern dash against Northern pluck and endurance." Despite the brief gap in the Union front caused by Prentiss's surrender, Grant's line held, though driven to the banks of the Tennessee.[15]

In assessing the outcome of the day, Grant gave much credit to Sherman for holding on until evening, when night, disorganization of troops, the death of Johnston, and Union gunboats finally halted the Confederate onslaught. Grant said he never felt the need to stay long in Sherman's sector, for he saw that his friend had everything under control and inspired his beleaguered troops to maintain a battlefront. McClernand, likewise, supposedly told Grant that Sherman's presence on the field made a key difference in favor of the Union. Sherman was slightly wounded but was able to remain in the fight. Grant shuddered to think what might have happened had he lost Sherman's leadership; "that day would have been a sad one for the troops engaged at Shiloh."[16]

While generous with praise for Sherman, Grant in his memoirs unfairly criticized Prentiss for not withdrawing with the rest of the Union line, since his failure to do so exposed his flanks and contributed to the mass surrender. Making such a case, when Grant knew he had urged Prentiss to hold his position, was disingenuous; whether or not it was an honest one, this assessment sounded like an effort to divert blame for the capture of so many men. Prentiss no doubt did stay in place too long, but Grant could have shown more understanding of the sacrifice that he and the other captives made.[17]

During the fighting, Grant rode back to the Tennessee to check on Buell, who, given their probable earlier disagreement about enemy threats at Nashville, may have felt some sense of justice at seeing Grant squirm. Grant later remembered that when he found Buell, "there probably were as many as four or five thousand stragglers lying under cover of the river bluff, panic-stricken, most of whom would have been shot where they lay, without resistance, before they would have taken muskets and marched to the front to protect themselves." Talking with Buell on a dispatch boat, Grant urged him to get his troops across the river as soon as possible. As

he left, Grant observed that Buell was exhorting and even threatening with naval shells the slackers who had fled the battlefield.
His threats fell on deaf ears, for these were not his men, and anyway, they were too terrified to be intimidated by any officer.[18]

As the fighting closed for the day, Grant and his staff assessed
their situation. A line of artillery was deployed along the bluff of
the river, with one intact division, commanded by Stephen Hurlbut,
providing support. On Hurlbut's right, McClernand and Sherman
tried to bring some semblance of order to their divisions. W. H. L.
Wallace's troops, their commander mortally wounded, had become
so disorganized that Grant no longer considered them a viable division. Sherman held a bridge until Lew Wallace finally arrived
that night, crossed a creek, and deployed his troops on Sherman's
right. Meanwhile, Union gunboats and the line of artillery held back
Confederate attempts to turn Grant's left.

Grant, who had maintained a steadying influence during the
fighting, keeping hidden whatever trepidations he may have felt,
spent the evening encouraging his division commanders, reminding them of his successful advance on Fort Donelson. Miffed at
Buell's slowness, he thought that Lew Wallace's presence would
ensure victory on the morrow, regardless of Buell's possible contri-
bution. Buell's army took over the Union left, however, and the
Federal forces positioned themselves for a counterattack the next
day. Heavy rain made the night miserable for both armies. Grant's
injured ankle was so swollen and painful that he retreated to a log
cabin serving as a hospital close to the river, but the sights and
sounds of amputations and other surgeries soon drove him back
into the rain, where he found shelter under a tree. After dark the
Confederates, now commanded by P. G. T. Beauregard, had pulled
back to reorganize, to escape gunboat and Union artillery fire, and
to take advantage of abandoned enemy tents that offered protection from the rain.[19]

Next morning, April 7, Grant prepared to give the enemy what
his troops had experienced the day before. His line from right to
left, included the divisions of Lew Wallace, Sherman, McClernand,
and Hurlbut and Buell's Army of the Ohio. Grant, in effect, had
two armies now on the field, his own and Buell's. Throughout the
day the reinforced Union line pushed back the Confederates, who
had no reinforcements, for Van Dorn had not yet arrived. Grant
narrowly escaped injury when a bullet hit "the metal scabbard of
my sword, just below the hilt." About midafternoon, noticing an

opening in the enemy line between Sherman and McClernand, Grant gathered some troops, "formed them in line of battle and marched them forward, going in front [himself] to prevent premature or long-range firing." When the troops got close to the Rebels, Grant rode to the side; a charge was ordered, and the disheartened Confederates broke. Soon, Beauregard's fatigued army was streaming back toward Corinth.[20]

Don Carlos Buell. From Ezra J. Warner, *Generals in Blue: Lives of the Union Commanders* (Baton Rouge: Louisiana State University Press, 1964), 51.

The victorious Federals did not pursue aggressively. Grant sent Sherman with a detachment of cavalry and infantry after the Confederates, but Rebel rearguard resistance by Bedford Forrest's cavalry ended this limited action. Grant later claimed that he truly wanted to press the Rebels "but had not the heart to order the men who had fought desperately for two days, lying in the mud and rain whenever not fighting, and I did not feel disposed to positively order Buell, or any part of his command, to pursue." No doubt many of the men were worn down; they had participated in the bloodiest battle of the war up to that time, and victory had not come easily.[21] Still, Grant's words ring hollow. He was senior in rank to Buell and certainly had the right to issue a pursuit order, though Grant wrote, unconvincingly, in his memoirs that Buell had recently been a departmental commander, while he himself had "commanded only a district." Apparently, he either felt a bit intimidated or did not trust Buell to carry out the pursuit of Beauregard. Grant further stated that by the time he actually saw Buell again, it may have been too late to put together an effective advance; had he found Buell at the "moment of the last charge," he wrote, "I should have at least requested him to follow."[22]

A more realistic assessment could be that Grant was simply in no mood to send his army south. Johnston's attack had thoroughly shocked him, and he had spent many anxious hours on April 6 looking for reinforcements and wondering whether his army could survive the day's assault. That anxiety, his injured ankle, the miserable night of the sixth, and the sights and sounds of a field hospital had undoubtedly influenced his thinking. His overconfidence at Pittsburg Landing had almost cost him dearly and indeed *had* cost the Union more than 13,000 total casualties—nearly 11,000 of those from his Army of the Tennessee—while the Confederates counted just over 10,500 losses. Yet he had won the day on April 7, and he had done so with Buell's and Wallace's fresh troops. From those ranks a pursuit force could have been pulled and sent after Beauregard, perhaps with very telling effect. But Grant's usual aggressive psyche had been suppressed by the action at Shiloh, and despite his later rationalizations, he simply had no fight in him and concluded that continuing after the Rebels would be unfair to his army. What might have happened had he followed the Confederates and inflicted more damage can never be known, but the forthcoming Corinth campaign might have been unnecessary.

Shiloh weighed heavily on Grant's mind long after the battle, and he spent a few pages of his memoirs addressing the subsequent criticism of his leadership and his later removal as commander of troops at Pittsburg Landing. He defended the army's lack of entrenchments by pointing out that his men needed to drill more than they needed to dig fortifications, and obviously he felt they did not have time to do both. "Up to that time," he wrote, "the pick and spade had been but little resorted to at the West." His words indicate that he did not think in terms of protecting his troops with entrenchments. "Contrary to all my experience up to that time," he pointed out, "and to the experience of the army I was then commanding, we were on the defensive. We were without intrenchments or defensive advantages of any sort."[23] Grant never changed his mind about fortifications—he always preferred being on the offensive—but in upcoming campaigns he did learn the value of well-constructed earthworks. The beating his army took at Shiloh, and the campaign of criticism waged against him in the aftermath, shifted his demeanor toward very uncharacteristic timidity that became more and more apparent in the following months, but he never embraced the pick and shovel as weapons of war.

Shiloh also affected Grant's concept of the war overall, particularly what it would take to win. After the performance of Johnston's and Beauregard's Confederates, Grant "gave up all idea of saving the Union except by complete conquest." He still preferred a soft approach to civilians but modified his insistence that all local noncombatants, wherever their allegiance lay, must have their personal property protected against any sort of vandalism by Federal troops. After Shiloh, he "regarded it as humane to both sides to protect the persons of those found at their homes, but to consume everything that could be used to support or supply armies. Protection was still continued over such supplies as were within lines held by us and which we expected to continue to hold; but such supplies within the reach of Confederate armies I regarded as much contraband as arms or ordnance stores." Although he continued to warn against pillaging by his soldiers and to punish offenders, he wrestled more and more with the issue of hard war as the fighting dragged on. Despite his protestations to the contrary, he and other Union officers eventually ignored the destruction of private property wrought by his troops.[24]

Shiloh further brought about the most frustrating and depressing few weeks of Grant's Civil War career. He wrote no formal report of the battle to Henry Halleck, largely because he learned that Buell and his subordinates had bypassed him and sent reports directly to Halleck. Their doing so was not as great a slight as it seemed to Grant; Buell did, after all, command a separate army and had been reporting to Halleck before Shiloh. Grant reasoned, however, that he could not write his own report without access to the reports of all the generals in the battle. Halleck claimed to understand Grant's position but said that all paperwork received had already been forwarded to Washington, so Grant could not review what had been written. Aside from Grant's rather terse comments about the episode in his memoirs, however, there is no written evidence that this incident added to the ill will between him and Halleck.[25]

Ultimately, the wrangle over battle reports did not seem to matter to Grant's career, for Halleck moved his headquarters from St. Louis to Pittsburg Landing and took personal command of both Grant's and Buell's troops. His arrival was rooted in a storm of widespread condemnation of Grant's performance at Shiloh, despite his victory. If Grant had had trouble recovering from the sting of the battle itself, he had much more to endure as a wave of calls for his dismissal swept the North, reaching all the way to the White House.

How Grant's own men reacted to Shiloh has not been well documented, and perhaps the survivors were so worn by the fighting that most did not immediately write down their thoughts. Many must surely have wondered, as did many beyond the battlefield, why their leaders had not prepared them for an enemy attack. Some said so, blaming the bloodshed on their commanders' incompetence. The shock of a battle of this magnitude, which left in its wake thousands of mangled wounded and dead bodies, took time to sink in. Grant's image among his troops had been tarnished, and he would have to work hard to regain their respect as well as his self-confidence.

The Union's 13,000 casualties horrified its citizens and the Lincoln government, and newspapers in the North berated Grant for not being prepared for the Confederate attack. Republicans assailed Grant, and even his supporters had trouble defending his absence from the field when the shooting began. Old stories of his heavy prewar drinking immediately surfaced. But Henry Halleck, prompted by Washington to examine the situation, did not take this obvious chance to suggest Grant's removal from command; with his personal investigation revealing no gross misconduct on Grant's part, he decided not to join the general's most vocal critics.

Why Halleck backed away from an opportunity to get rid of Grant can be surmised only from other factors. Beyond finding nothing egregious in Grant's conduct, he may have been unwilling to take on Grant's supporters, including some who had more influence in Washington than he did. Grant's old friend, Congressman Washburne, came to his defense, even as some of Lincoln's advisers pushed for removal, fearing political damage if the president did not act. Lincoln, however, supposedly responded to such cries, "I can't spare this man; he fights." Although Grant had made some obvious mistakes, he indeed had shown a resolve to fight back rather than quit. He had done so at Donelson, and he had not cowered after the first day at Shiloh. He had fought and won, and whatever the depth of disdain Halleck may have had for Grant's performance, he understood that in battle, victory mattered most of all. Grant was the kind of general the Union needed, and Lincoln was wise enough to know it. Perhaps it is more reasonable to assert that since Halleck found nothing in the evidence to support bringing charges against Grant, neither did Lincoln. Halleck may have suggested a simple demotion to appease the critics, for that is what happened next. Lincoln agreed with the decision, and his advisers supported the move as a way to undercut continuing attacks on Grant.[26]

Halleck gathered three armies at Pittsburg Landing: John Pope's Army of the Mississippi, fresh from capturing Island No. 10 on the Mississippi; Buell's Army of the Ohio; and the Army of the Tennessee, now commanded by George H. Thomas. Grant was placed second in command to Halleck, though ostensibly in command of the army's right wing, his Army of the Tennessee. Halleck seemed to enjoy occasionally lording his authority over Grant, as when he pointed out on April 14 that the army was in poor condition to withstand an attack, implying that this situation was due to Grant's inadequate leadership. In actual practice, Grant found himself being "little more than an observer. Orders were sent direct to the right wing or reserve, ignoring me," he worte, "and advances were made from one line of intrenchments to another without notifying me. My position was so embarrassing in fact that I made several applications . . . to be relieved." Any advice he gave Halleck was summarily ignored until after Corinth was occupied. Then Grant was given permission to leave the department, but Sherman encouraged him to stay, and he did, giving up his hope for a new assignment.[27]

Sherman recalled Grant's comment that he was little more than "in the way here. I have stood it as long as I can, and can endure it no longer." Sherman "begged him to stay, illustrating his case by my own": before Shiloh, newspapers had printed assertions that

Sherman had lost his mind, but a "single battle had given me new life." He reasoned that if Grant went away, "events would go right along, and he would be left out; whereas, if he remained, some happy accident might restore him to favor and his true place." Whether Grant relished waiting for a "happy accident" or not, he appreciated the advice and, fortunately for the Union cause, decided to endure, which he did better than anything else.[28]

Grant wondered where his endurance would ultimately lead. When he objected to his situation, he received a curt reply from Halleck:

> I am very much surprised, general, that you should find any cause of complaint in the recent assignment of commands. You have precisely the position to which your rank entitles you. Had I given you the right wing or reserve only it would have been a reduction rather than increase of command, and I could not give you both without placing you in the position you now occupy. You certainly will not suspect me of any intention to injure your feelings or reputation or to do you any injustice; if so, you will eventually change your mind on this subject. For the last three months I have done everything in my power to ward off the attacks which were made upon you. If you believe me your friend you will not require explanations; if not, explanations on my part would be of little avail.

Grant must have shaken his head in wonder at these words. With such a friend, he needed no enemies.[29]

Both public and official reactions no doubt added to Grant's tendency toward tentative behavior during the coming weeks. He had survived and would eventually regain his command when Halleck was called to Washington to become general in chief of the armies, but he had learned the price of perceived failure and learned further that people would take his scalp, if they could, for political or military reasons or both. His subordinate John McClernand, seeing an opportunity to use his beleaguered commander's condemnation to further his own career, had colored his report of Shiloh to make himself look better than was warranted. Grant filed away this kind of backstabbing in his mind, never forgetting whom he could and could not trust. He had taken some hard knocks, and as Halleck led the massive Union army very slowly and methodically toward Mississippi, Grant had plenty of time to analyze them, since his new duties were so few. The aggressive, offensive-minded general who had arrived at Pittsburg Landing full of energy and confi-

U. S. Grant, ca. 1862. *Courtesy of Vicksburg National Military Park*

dence now felt beaten down and bridled. From the highs of triumph on the Tennessee and the Cumberland he had fallen to a point
so low that transfer or perhaps resignation seemed an attractive
option. John Pope noticed how "silent and brooding" Grant became, and how during those dark days "when he spoke at all, it

was to talk of resigning." Only time and Sherman convinced him not to do so.[30]

In truth, Grant had both violated the tenets that had served him well before Shiloh and fallen victim to the same shortcomings. Halleck had ordered him to wait for Buell, and he had done so, and the delay had been costly; the earlier Grant would not have been so willing to let a distant superior hold him back. Perhaps his bad experience with Halleck after Donelson had had more impact than he would have admitted. Of course, whatever role his reluctance to cross his superior may have played, Grant's certainty that the Rebels would not attack made him feel no need to rush into action without Buell. He had not worried about what he could not see, and his army had paid dearly for that carelessness. The navy had once again served him well, even though its participation had not been planned: naval guns had helped bring to a halt the first day's Confederate push.

Still, it was Grant's determination not to give up but to keep on fighting that likely saved his career. He had ordered a counterattack, rather than withdrawing as some generals had done already in similar circumstances, notably in Virginia. Whatever tribulations he faced were mild compared to what must surely have happened had he ordered a withdrawal and left the battlefield in Confederate hands. Somewhere beneath his humiliation, the combative Sam Grant remained, and only time would tell whether that part of him could resurface.

NOTES

1. Grant, *Memoirs*, 222.
2. Ibid., 223; Herman L. Hattaway and Archer Jones, *How the North Won: A Military History of the Civil War* (Urbana, IL, 1983), 156–57, 161.
3. OR, ser. 1, vol. 10, pt. 2, pp. 41–55; Grant, *Memoirs*, 223.
4. Grant, *Memoirs*, 223–24; Larry J. Daniel, *Shiloh: The Battle That Changed the Civil War* (New York, 1997), 132; Simon, *Papers of Grant*, 5:14.
5. Grant, *Memoirs*, 224.
6. Ibid.; OR, ser. 1, vol. 10, pt. 2, p. 91.
7. Grant, *Memoirs*, 224–25; Simpson, *Grant*, 136.
8. Grant, *Memoirs*, 225; OR, ser. 1, vol. 10, pt. 2, pp. 91–92, 94.
9. Grant, *Memoirs*, 225–26; Daniel, *Shiloh*, 174.
10. Grant, *Memoirs*, 226.
11. Ibid., 226–27.
12. Daniel, *Shiloh*, 175–76; OR, ser. 1, vol. 10, pt. 1, p. 250.
13. Grant, *Memoirs*, 227; OR, ser. 1, vol. 10, pt. 1, p. 387.
14. Daniel, *Shiloh*, 203; OR, ser. 1,vol. 10, pt. 1, pp. 278–79.

15. Grant, *Memoirs*, 228.
16. Ibid., 231; *OR*, ser. 1, vol. 10, pt. 1, p. 117.
17. Grant, *Memoirs*, 228.
18. Ibid., 231–32; *OR*, ser. 1, vol. 10, pt. 1, p. 292.
19. Grant, *Memoirs*, 232–35; Daniel, *Shiloh*, 266.
20. Grant, *Memoirs*, 236–37; John F. Marszalek, *Sherman: A Soldier's Passion for Order* (New York, 1993), 180.
21. Grant, *Memoirs*, 237–38.
22. Ibid.; Daniel, *Shiloh*, 322.
23. Simpson, *Grant*, 129; Grant, *Memoirs*, 239.
24. Grant, *Memoirs*, 246; Mark Grimsley, *The Hard Hand of War: Union Military Policy toward Southern Civilians* (New York, 1995), chap. 5.
25. Grant, *Memoirs*, 247–48; Stephen D. Engle, *Don Carlos Buell: Most Promising of All* (Chapel Hill, NC, 1999), 238.
26. Daniel, *Shiloh*, 298–99, 304–9; Simpson, *Grant*, 136–37; Engle, *Buell*, 236; Wiley Sword, *Shiloh: Bloody April* (New York, 1974), 434.
27. Grant, *Memoirs*, 248, 251; *OR*, ser. 1, vol. 10, pt. 2, pp. 105–6.
28. William T. Sherman, *Memoirs of William T. Sherman*, 2 vols. in one (New York, 1994), 188–89; Grant, *Memoirs*, 258.
29. *OR*, ser. 1, vol. 10, pt. 2, pp. 182–83.
30. Peter Cozzens, *The Darkest Days of the War: Battles of Iuka and Corinth* (Chapel Hill, NC, 1997), 17.

CHAPTER FIVE

SECURING NORTHERN MISSISSIPPI

GENERAL P. G. T. BEAUREGARD evacuated Corinth on May 29, 1862, right under Henry Halleck's nose. While Halleck anticipated Confederate attacks, Beauregard withdrew his army south to the Tupelo, Mississippi, area. U. S. Grant endorsed Halleck's snail-like pursuit of the Rebels at the time, but with the benefit of hindsight he later bemoaned the boost to enemy morale wrought by Beauregard's uncontested retreat and the halfhearted pursuit by Pope and Buell that availed Union forces nothing. The occupation of Corinth did give Federal troops strategic advantages, but Grant and other officers "could not see how the mere occupation of places was to close the war while large and effective rebel armies existed." Halleck, on the other hand, "unnerved by the mess he found at Pittsburg Landing," had intentionally moved at a "tediously slow" pace and was satisfied with the taking of Corinth. Grant had to be content with commanding the District of West Tennessee, an assignment he received on July 17 and found very unchallenging.[1]

To make matters worse, once Halleck put men to work digging fortifications around Corinth, the dispersal of the huge Federal army began. With calls for help amid warnings of Confederate operations in the region, Halleck felt obligated to send Buell east to take Chattanooga and challenge Braxton Bragg, who had replaced Beauregard and had taken a large detachment of the Shiloh/Corinth army east to threaten Middle Tennessee. John Pope was called to Virginia to see if he could handle Robert E. Lee and, at Second Manassas, proved he could not. Pope's wing that remained behind was scattered along the Tennessee-Mississippi border, and other reinforcements went to Arkansas.[2]

While he marked time along with the rest of the Federal army, Grant familiarized himself with the territory between Corinth and Memphis, which city officials had surrendered to the Union on June 6. Grant listened to the complaints of some citizens regarding their treatment by the invading Yankees, but he had no sympathy for Southerners who protested the inconveniences of a war they themselves had started. He worried about his own future, for he feared being relegated to the backwater of the war for its duration. A turning point finally came when Henry Halleck left for Washington in mid-July to assume the duties of commanding general of U.S. armies, paving the way for Grant to take over the Department of the Mississippi. He did not do so officially, however, until October 25, an indication that the powers in Washington still considered him to be on probation. During the intervening period, his de facto command of the department had not given him any sense of security.[3]

Supposedly, Halleck considered putting someone else in charge. A story eventually surfaced that he had offered the job to a quartermaster officer named Robert Allen, who held only the rank of colonel but was a friend of Halleck. Allen turned down the position, apparently thinking his rank did not qualify him for such a promotion and preferring to stay where he was. If true, this episode underscored Halleck's continuing lack of respect for Grant. Though he makes no mention of Allen in his memoirs, army gossip being what it has always been, Grant would have known about such an offer, but he did not let it affect his future dealings with Halleck.[4]

In fact, Grant wrote to his political shield, Elihu Washburne, in glowing terms about Halleck's ability, words perhaps intended to prove to Washburne and, by extension, official Washington that he still considered himself a team player and bore no ill will. Or perhaps he genuinely felt no bitterness; he would not learn until years afterward that Halleck had earlier sent critical messages about him to the War Department. In his memoir, Grant chose not to comment further. Or perhaps ignorance truly was bliss, for if Grant had been critical of Halleck's promotion, his own future in the army might have been more uncertain. As it was, his warm words for Halleck, plus other comments, such as his views about a soldier's duties—"He is to obey the orders of all those placed over him and whip the enemy wherever he meets him"—surely brightened his image, making it easy for Washburne to praise and defend him.[5]

Although back in official command at last in October, Grant inherited a situation that gave him little reason for optimism. The dissolution of an army that had once numbered 120,000 was so complete that Union forces still stationed along the Corinth-Memphis corridor seemed to be in a precarious position: "I was put entirely on the defensive in a territory whose population was hostile to the Union." Troops constructed additional defensive positions at

Corinth, which, given its strategic railroad crossing, had to be held to secure Federal deployments. Grant positioned troops to protect his northern and eastern flanks, and he felt he had sufficient strength between Corinth and Memphis to protect the former from the west and to secure the latter. Corinth's potential vulnerabilities lay to the south and, to a lesser extent, the east. He made sure that sufficient troops guarded the Mobile & Ohio Railroad and the Mississippi Central Railroad, which emerged from Mississippi and, running north into West Tennessee, were vital to Grant's overland supply routes from the North.[6]

To the south, Earl Van Dorn and Sterling Price presented a threat. Van Dorn commanded at Vicksburg, where in the late summer of 1862, efforts by the Union navy to capture that hill city on the Mississippi had failed. Price had been ordered to Mississippi from Missouri, and his troops hovered southwest of Iuka, a town on the Memphis & Charleston Railroad, which ran east from Memphis through Corinth and Iuka and on into Alabama. Van Dorn sent a force to recapture Baton Rouge, the Louisiana capital on the Mississippi, but in early August these troops were forced to retreat, thanks to the firepower of the Union navy. Van Dorn then decided to join Price in northern Mississippi; he had grandiose ideas of supporting Braxton Bragg's Tennessee operations by pushing Grant aside and racing through West Tennessee all the way into Kentucky. Buell, contesting Bragg's threats to Tennessee and Kentucky, expected Grant to make sure that Van Dorn and Price stayed put.[7]

Feeling undermanned and frustrated by having to remain on the defensive, which was contrary to his nature, Grant had to be satisfied with maintaining the status quo and monitoring the skirmishing, especially between opposing cavalry, that frequently broke out along the Mississippi-Tennessee border. Meanwhile, he dealt with the problem of continual discontent among local citizens. Many were helping the Rebels, both by transmitting information about Union operations and by funneling supplies southward. Washington pressured Grant to be tough in dealing with such people, but Grant was reluctant because he had trouble distinguishing between avid Rebel supporters and loyal citizens who had been pressured into providing Confederate support. He could be aggressive on the battlefield, but he continued to be reticent about confrontations with civilians.[8]

In late August and early September, action in northeastern Mississippi picked up. Grant's disposition of forces stretched from east of the Corinth area, where William Rosecrans commanded the left wing, back to Corinth, where E. O. C. Ord held the center, and west to Memphis, occupied by William T. Sherman's troops. Thanks to railroads, the telegraph, and couriers, Grant believed he had the information needed to dispatch troops quickly to any point of attack. Yet Confederate cavalryman Frank Armstrong demonstrated how easily the long Union line could be penetrated when he led a raid up the Mississippi Central Railroad to near Bolivar, Tennessee. Such events fueled Grant's fears that the Rebels intended to attack Corinth, and Halleck compounded his worries by insisting that Grant send first two divisions, then an additional one, to Buell. Unfortunately, Grant had earlier conceded that he thought Corinth was safe, so Halleck assumed that he could spare these men. (Grant learned through such incidents to be candid with Halleck rather than tell him what Grant thought he wanted to hear.) Now, when Grant complained, Halleck gave him permission to give up Corinth if necessary, clearly deeming Buell's efforts to stop Bragg in Tennessee the higher priority.[9]

To the south, Price was being pressured by Bragg to move northeast toward Iuka to prevent Grant from sending reinforcements to Tennessee. Since Grant had been ordered to keep Price and Van Dorn from reinforcing Bragg, a situation emerged in which two forces, each determined to keep the other from going to Tennessee, seemed headed toward a showdown. Grant sent William Rosecrans to guard Eastport, located north of Iuka on the Tennessee River, a strategic landing that seemed for the moment to be a secure Union supply depot and a safe river embarkation point for transferring Union troops to Buell's aid in Tennessee. Since Eastport was not far from Iuka, Grant decided to deal with two issues in one operation: defeating Price would secure Eastport and keep Bragg from getting reinforcements from Mississippi.[10]

Grant's frame of mind during this period is significant. He may have entered the war with shadows of failure in civilian life hanging over him, but he had performed well, whatever his mistakes. His victory at Fort Donelson had brought him nationwide attention, but he had been humbled to the point of considering himself an outcast as a result of Shiloh. Despite his low-key demeanor, U. S. Grant had considerable pride in his abilities as a soldier, and the fall from the high of Fort Donelson to the low of Shiloh had been a plunge he would long remember. Halleck's departure for Washington had offered little respite, for Grant was still in a tenuous position, commanding a force he thought insufficient to take the offensive in a significant way. Nevertheless, he wanted to act, to chase away the lingering perceptions of incompetence that had been formed of him by the press and Halleck. Yet given his orders, he seemed destined to do little more than support Buell.

When he saw an opportunity to take to the field, then, Grant jumped at it, reverting to the impetuosity and overconfidence that could have cost him dearly at Belmont and had caught him by surprise at Donelson and Shiloh. In his zeal to polish his besmirched reputation, Grant formed a plan that was difficult to execute and, in the end, failed to achieve the victory he envisioned. Further, he seemed oddly detached, deciding to stay away from the battlefield himself and thereby exacerbating the difficulty of communications, already made tenuous enough by wet weather and difficult terrain.

Sterling Price's activities in early September convinced Grant that the Rebels intended either to attack Corinth, embark on some other movement to threaten the Union's northern Mississippi line, or send reinforcements to Bragg before Grant could stop them. Union scouts tried to track Price, and around September 11 they learned that the Rebels were moving toward Baldwyn and Bay Springs, north and northeast of Tupelo, respectively. Price wanted to prevent Rosecrans from reinforcing Buell, but also, if the opportunity arose, he wanted to go to Tennessee to join Bragg. Reports of Rosecrans's presence in the Iuka area clouded the picture for the Confederates, especially when Rosecrans moved west toward Corinth. Price advanced on Iuka, occupied it on September 14, and determined to stay there and block any Union attempt to send troops via rail to Buell. Meanwhile, Price encouraged Van Dorn to bring a portion of the Vicksburg army for a joint attack on Corinth. Grant thus had reason to be nervous about Confederate intentions. Whatever he decided, he certainly could not afford for his first post-Shiloh action to go against him.[11]

Grant sifted through his scouts' differing reports about Price's presence in Iuka. One piece of intelligence indicated that the Rebels planned to cross the Tennessee and move north into Kentucky. Other scouts believed that Van Dorn and Price were setting up a pincer movement against Corinth. A third notion was that Price would cross the Tennessee as a diversion to give Van Dorn a chance to attack distracted Federals at Corinth. After analyzing written and oral messages, Grant decided that Van Dorn, reportedly moving north with an army from the Vicksburg area, could not yet be close

William S. Rosecrans. From Ezra J. Warner, *Generals in Blue: Lives of the Union Commanders* (Baton Rouge: Louisiana State University Press, 1964), 410.

enough to constitute a threat. He thus chose to go after Price and beat him at Iuka before turning his attention to Van Dorn. Grant had tired of waiting; the enemy was at Iuka and must be attacked. Typically, he wanted to take the initiative and make it work in his favor. He did not intend to suffer the consequences of idleness, as he had at Shiloh.[12]

Grant's plan of operation, however, presented potential problems. Rosecrans marched south to the Rienzi area, turned east and then north, approaching Iuka from the south. Meanwhile, E. O. C. Ord led a separate wing east down the railroad to strike Iuka from the northwest. Reinforcements from Bolivar gave Grant some 17,000 men in the field, plus a sufficient force to protect Corinth. As Rosecrans marched, he dropped off detachments to check any Confederate attempt to approach Corinth from the south. Rosecrans moved eastward through Jacinto toward the southern approaches to Iuka with 9,000 troops; Ord took 8,000 east from Corinth. Price had some 14,000 in and around Iuka. The weather turned bad, with torrential rains slowing Rosecrans's pace.

Grant hoped to catch Price between the forces of Ord and Rosecrans—but how could their movements be coordinated? Everything depended upon having Rosecrans in place south of Iuka on the night of September 18 so that Ord could attack on the nineteenth. Once Price responded to Ord's assault, Rosecrans must hit the Confederate rear and destroy Price. The two Federal wings were miles apart, however, unable to communicate except by couriers riding hard and being careful not to get so close to Iuka that Price's pickets might see them and sound the alarm. An operation that depended upon such timing was risky at best, and Rosecrans's army was marching in miserable weather through unfamiliar territory, depending upon guides who might or might not be reliable. Grant had abandoned his usual practice of simple battle plans that could be plainly understood and easily carried out, yet the tactical aspects of the operation exhibited his favorite idea of diverting the enemy's attention with two wings, either one of which could launch a rear attack. On paper, the plan looked good, but the possibility of something going awry seemed very real.[13]

The effort to find guides who had an accurate knowledge of the area created problems very quickly. Sometime after midnight, September 18, Grant received a message from Rosecrans that because of delays, the south wing would not be in position at Iuka until around 1:00 or 2:00 P.M. on the nineteenth. In his after-action report, Grant noted his consternation: "Receiving this dispatch as I did late at night, and when I expected these troops were far on their way toward Iuka and had made plans accordingly, it caused some disappointment and made change of plan necessary. I immediately dispatched to General Ord, giving him the substance of the above and directions not to move on the enemy until Rosecrans

BATTLE OF IUKA
September 19, 1862

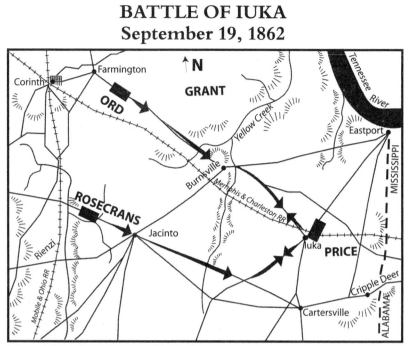

Adapted from Peter Cozzens, *The Darkest Days of the War: The Battles of Iuka and Corinth* (Chapel Hill: University of North Carolina Press, 1997), 69.

arrived or he should hear firing to the south of Iuka." Another messenger was sent to Rosecrans with these details. Ord, meanwhile, sent word through enemy lines to Price, informing him of Robert E. Lee's disastrous defeat in Maryland at Antietam and advising the Confederates to surrender. Price, of course, having no corroboration, rejected Ord's advice. (Antietam was actually a stalemate, not a smashing Union victory, as both sides at Iuka eventually learned.)[14]

Meanwhile, Rosecrans's advance moved to within 8 miles of Iuka by midnight, and he tried to inform Grant of his progress, but his message, given the courier's difficulties in riding through the night in dense woodland and through myriad streams and swampy bottomland, did not reach Grant until the next day—after Rosecrans had fought Price. Worse, Rosecrans had not received Grant's instruction that Ord was to wait for news of his arrival or sounds of battle before attacking; he expected Ord to take the lead in the battle as originally planned. Meanwhile, Grant and Ord met during the night and decided that Rosecrans would likely not be in a position

E. O. C. Ord. From Ezra J. Warner, *Generals in Blue: Lives of the Union Commanders* (Baton Rouge: Louisiana State University Press, 1964), 350.

to attack Price on the nineteenth; therefore, Ord should press Price's pickets, "but not . . . bring on an engagement unless he should hear firing." It is indeed odd, and perhaps indicative of Grant's worries about the outcome of the campaign, that he changed his plans without notifying Rosecrans. Coordination now seemed unlikely, with the two commanders operating under different scenarios.[15]

Rosecrans ran into Price's troops during the afternoon of September 19, and a bitter fight raged for hours south of Iuka, from around 2:30 P.M. until after dark. Rosecrans waited in vain for Ord to assault Price's rear, noting in his later report that he was "profoundly disappointed at hearing nothing from the forces on the Burnsville [Corinth] road." Price, now aware that he could be trapped between Union forces, withdrew to the south, past Rosecrans's battered wing. Ord later claimed that no sounds of fighting had reached him until the next morning. He explained why, in his opinion, he had not heard the noise of battle on the nineteenth and therefore had not rushed to Rosecrans's aid: "The wind freshly blowing from us in the direction of Iuka during the whole of the 19th, prevented our hearing the guns and co-operating with General Rosecrans." A recent explanation has partially confirmed Ord's analysis: perhaps an acoustical phenomenon created by a combination of geographic, atmospheric, and wind conditions, especially "damp air", did combine to keep sounds of battle from reaching Ord's position. Cynics, however, once again, brought up Grant's drinking reputation and claimed that he and possibly others were too drunk to hear artillery and small arms fire. There is no credible evidence of any such circumstance.[16]

Grant had little sympathy for Rosecrans's predicament, though he had likewise heard nothing of the fighting on the nineteenth from his headquarters at Burnsville. Not until 8:35 A.M. the next day did Grant receive word of the previous evening's conflict in a dispatch that Rosecrans had written at 10:30 P.M. (The time that messengers took to get from Rosecrans to Grant demonstrated the communications problem.) Grant immediately ordered Ord to the assault, but it came too late to catch Price. Rosecrans's failure to secure the Iuka-Fulton road, by which Price made his withdrawal, infuriated Grant. "Our only defeat," he claimed after Iuka, "was in not capturing the entire army or in destroying it as I had hoped to do." Grant's tendency to place complete trust in his lieutenants, an admirable trait in some ways, occasionally backfired. He expected Rosecrans to get the job done, and when that did not happen, he uncharacteristically criticized rather than pausing to analyze. His blaming others was no doubt a direct result of his post-Shiloh experience: in his haste to protect himself from potential criticism over Price's escape, he treated Rosecrans just as he himself had been treated by critics rushing to judgment just a few months earlier.[17]

In his memoirs, Grant embraced Ord's acoustical explanation as to why neither he nor Ord became aware of the September 19 fighting. He recalled further his dismay at finding that Price had escaped. He ordered Rosecrans to pursue him and rode along with his subordinate to see that the order was executed, then came back to Iuka. He learned later that Rosecrans "followed only a few miles after I left him and then went into camp, and the pursuit was continued no further. I was disappointed at the result of the battle of Iuka—but I had so high an opinion of General Rosecrans that I found no fault at the time." In fact, Grant did find fault at the time; he just chose not to make a major issue of it. As for Rosecrans, when he learned from Ord about the change of plans the night of September 18, he became so infuriated that his relationship with Grant suffered irreparable damage.[18]

Grant's hopes for a smashing victory had ended in chagrin. He seemed still to be floundering in his efforts to regain his self-confidence and his stature as the hero of Fort Donelson. He had made poor decisions, both in composing complicated plans that could, and did, easily go wrong and in his failure to recognize communications problems that proved impossible to overcome. In setting up his headquarters at Burnsville, he seemed almost intentionally to distance himself from the action, a decision that went against his normally aggressive behavior. His post-Shiloh depression apparently had not altogether left him, and although he seemed eager to defeat Price, when the time came to go into action he pulled back, perhaps fearing another setback. He had accomplished one of his aims: Price did not go to Bragg—but his escape led to his joining forces with Van Dorn. The fight at Iuka had set up another confrontation that would not be long in coming.

Grant during this period of the war was not the Grant before Shiloh or the Grant to come. From a general who refused to turn back, who stayed aggressive and never quit, he had evolved into a tentative officer who seemed terrified of failing. He physically absented himself from the battlefield, rather than leading by example. When Iuka did not turn out as he hoped, he pointed fingers of blame rather than accepting responsibility. Fortunately for the Union cause, this interim Grant soon overcame his worries, fears, and reluctance and became again the pre-Shiloh general.

In the aftermath of Iuka, Grant divided his district into four departments, appointed commanders for each, and felt some degree of security when Van Dorn showed no inclination to go on the offensive. Then he left for St. Louis, where his wife was living, ostensibly to confer with Samuel Curtis, commander of the Department of the Missouri, about reports of Rebel ironclads being constructed on the Yazoo River in central Mississippi and to talk about sending detachments to check on the rumors (which turned out to be untrue). That was his official reason for going to St. Louis, and a valid one, but perhaps there were others. Grant may well have wanted to get away from the frustrations of being on the defensive. He also had lingering though not serious health problems, probably brought on by stress. And he no doubt missed Julia, whose support and reassurances he needed and who had spent so much time with him that her absence exacerbated his disappointments and uncertainties.[19]

By the time he returned about five days later, Van Dorn and Price had merged their troops. Van Dorn, assuming overall command, wanted Corinth but chose to move north into West Tennessee as a ruse before turning southeast to attack the town from the northwest. As soon as Grant arrived back in Tennessee, he acted to counter Van Dorn's movements. Grant still felt isolated, forgotten by Washington. And, he later recalled, "We were in a country where nearly all the people, except the Negroes, were hostile to us and friendly to the cause we were trying to suppress. It was easy, therefore, for the enemy to get early information of our every move. We, on the contrary, had to go after our information in force, and then often returned without it." He tired, too, of Halleck's persistent requests to send detachments to investigate the rumors of Rebel ironclad construction on the Yazoo. Grant insisted that if he sent troops, he must have more to take their place; he had no desire to spread his forces thin, as Halleck had done. Grant further grumbled about not having any command authority across the Mississippi. Van Dorn's diversionary tactics convinced him for a time that the Rebels were headed north of Memphis, and he knew that Union troops across the river in Arkansas, over which he had no control, could be a big help in repelling such an enemy operation.[20]

While Grant was gradually realizing what Van Dorn truly intended, the Confederates marched on Corinth, where they attacked Rosecrans on October 3. Grant had written very apprehensively to Halleck two days earlier, "My position is precarious, but hope to get out of it all right." He sent reinforcements to Rosecrans from Stephen Hurlbut and James McPherson; Ord commanded Hurlbut's troops, which arrived too late for the fighting at Corinth. Rosecrans's well-entrenched army repulsed Van Dorn's poorly co-ordinated attacks on the third and fourth, and Ord was in a posi-tion to cut off Van Dorn's retreat west toward the Hatchie River, but an old road to the southwest allowed the Confederates to es-cape, and a strong Rebel rearguard held off Union troops at the Tuscumbia River.[21]

Despite his obvious success at Corinth itself, Rosecrans's ac-tions angered Grant. Rosecrans had allowed Price to escape at Iuka, and now Van Dorn was not pursued. Grant decried Rosecrans's failure "to follow up the victory, although I had given specific or-ders in advance of the battle for him to pursue the moment the enemy was repelled. He did not do so, and I repeated the order after the battle." When he did take up pursuit the next day, Grant complained, Rosecrans chose the wrong road, one that took him away from Van Dorn's route.[22] Rosecrans corrected the error and kept after Van Dorn all the way to Ripley. But then Grant deter-mined to recall him, later stating, "Had he gone much farther he would have met a greater force than Van Dorn had at Corinth and behind intrenchments or on chosen ground and the probabilities are he would have lost his army."[23]

These words in his memoirs are untrue, and indeed Grant knew shortly after the fact that he had acted too hastily. Reports indi-cated that no great reinforcements awaited Van Dorn and that had Rosecrans continued, he might very well have bagged Van Dorn and his army. Halleck wondered at Grant's decision but refused to order him to let Rosecrans go on, since Grant was the one on the scene and more aware of the situation. A furious Rosecrans always believed that he not only could have brought Van Dorn to heel but that the Union army could then have marched unfettered to Vicksburg. He was being overly optimistic, but he had something to prove and was sure that a golden opportunity had been denied him. He did not care what Grant thought but was furious with of-ficial Washington about a promotion slight that placed him lower on the seniority list than he thought was justified. Despite reassur-ances from Halleck that he had not been personally slighted but was merely a victim of circumstance, Rosecrans was a general with a mission, and Grant's recall of his pursuit of Van Dorn made him very bitter.[24]

Had U. S. Grant lost his nerve? Did he fear that Rosecrans would meet disaster, or was he just afraid to risk the army? His relationship with Rosecrans had deteriorated ever since the Iuka campaign, and he was frustrated with Rosecrans's initially hesitant pursuit. It was certainly true that Rosecrans's army had been in a hot two-day fight, and concerns about the limits of its endurance were valid, yet the euphoria of victory no doubt overrode much of their weariness. Perhaps Grant simply had lost trust in Rosecrans after Iuka, and perhaps, too, he was unwilling to risk a catastrophe to the army for which he would be blamed and possibly removed from command. With back-to-back victories on his record to help overcome the stain of the post-Shiloh period, why take the chance? Nevertheless, one must wonder if the pre-Shiloh Grant would have been so quick to let an enemy army go in peace. Probably not, and certainly the Grant of later Vicksburg fame would not have permitted such an opportunity to pass by. Grant simply had not emerged from his Shiloh funk to the point of being the aggressive general he had been and would be again.

He did enjoy some rewards of the two victories within his department. Halleck and Lincoln were both pleased; Halleck wished other Union leaders could accomplish as much, and Lincoln congratulated him via telegraph. As a result, Grant felt so upbeat that he predicted there would now be little fighting left to do to end the war in his department. Such "unwarranted optimism" had no foundation, for there was, in fact, much fighting left to do. But Grant had been under a cloud for so long that he grabbed at the chance to feel good about himself and his army's victories in northern Mississippi.[25]

Once the Iuka-Corinth campaign in the fall of 1862 had stabilized the Union front between Corinth and Memphis, Grant had to consider what to do next. With Van Dorn's army battered, the time seemed ripe for going on the offensive; Union soldiers who had won the two battles felt renewed enthusiasm and were ready to continue fighting; morale was on the rise in Grant's department. But all the troops he had sent to Tennessee convinced him that he must have reinforcements before he could launch any invasion deeper into Mississippi. He remained hesitant, his self-confidence still mired deeply in his Shiloh experience, and his relationship with many of his subordinates either shaky or based on lack of familiarity with their abilities. Grant trusted Sherman and had come to trust McPherson, whose engineering skills he much admired; in fact, he asked Halleck to have McPherson promoted to major general. On the negative side, Grant lost Ord, whom he had found dependable, for Ord had to leave active duty for a time to recuperate from serious wounds received at the Hatchie River.

In many ways, to use a modern sports metaphor, Grant was a quarterback in search of a team. He had had a taste of good teamwork in his early campaigns, but coordination had eluded his efforts at Shiloh and had been missing at Iuka and Corinth. The relations between commanders that he hoped for were evident in his report on Ord's and Hurlbut's actions during the aftermath of the fighting at Corinth. "Between them there should be, and I trust is, the warmest bonds of brotherhood. Each was risking life in the same cause, and on this occasion risking it also to save and assist each other." As the winter of 1862–63 approached, U. S. Grant longed for that kind of cooperation in his department and especially among his immediate lieutenants. Yet with his own post-Shiloh doubts and fears still plaguing him, he did very little himself to promote the kind of harmony and trust he sought. A commander's attitudes often spread to his subordinates, and in Grant's case, that could only result in shared uneasiness rather than mutual confidence. He was still groping for an opportunity to be the strong, effective leader of a strong army team that he had been early in the war. Iuka and Corinth allowed him a new start, but the challenges that awaited him would test his ability to mold an effective force of officers and men.[26]

NOTES

1. Grant, *Memoirs*, 255–56; Simpson, *Grant*, 142, 147; Daniel, *Shiloh*, 311.
2. Cozzens, *Darkest Days*, 32–33.
3. Grant, *Memoirs*, 261–63.
4. Badeau, *Grant*, 1:107–8. There is no consensus among Grant's recent biographers about the truth of the story. McFeely ignores it; Simpson, *Grant*, 146, apparently accepts it; and Jean Edward Smith, *Grant* (New York, 2001), 660 n. 69, rejects it.
5. Simon, *Papers of Grant*, 5:145–46; McFeely, *Grant*, 120.
6. Grant, *Memoirs*, 263–64.
7. See Cozzens, *Darkest Days*, 38–49.
8. Grant, *Memoirs*, 264–66.
9. Cozzens, *Darkest Days*, 46–48.
10. Ibid., 51.
11. Ibid., 50–60; Grant, *Memoirs*, 270.
12. Grant, *Memoirs*, 272; Cozzens, *Darkest Days*, 61; Simon, *Papers of Grant*, 6:38–42.
13. Cozzens, *Darkest Days*, 63–65; E. B. Long, *The Civil War Day by Day: An Almanac, 1861–1865* (New York, 1971), 269; Grant, *Memoirs*, 272.

14. Simpson, *Grant*, 151; Cozzens, *Darkest Days*, 70; *OR*, ser. 1, vol. 17, pt. 1, p. 67.

15. *OR*, ser. 1, vol. 17, pt. 1, p. 67.

16. Cozzens, *Darkest Days*, 129–30; *OR*, ser. 1, vol. 17, pt. 1, pp. 74, 119.

17. *OR*, ser. 1, vol. 17, pt. 1, pp. 67–68.

18. Grant, *Memoirs*, 276–77; Cozzens, *Darkest Days*, 126.

19. *OR*, ser. 1, vol. 17, pt. 2, p. 235; Simpson, *Grant*, 154.

20. Grant, *Memoirs*, 278–79; Cozzens, *Darkest Days*, 148; *OR*, ser. 1, vol. 17, pt. 2, pp. 240–41.

21. Grant, *Memoirs*, 279; *OR*, ser. 1, vol. 17, pt. 2, p. 250.

22. Grant, *Memoirs*, 280.

23. Ibid., 281.

24. Cozzens, *Darkest Days*, 303–4; *OR*, ser. 1, vol. 17, pt. 2, p. 239.

25. Simpson, *Grant*, 155; Basler, *Lincoln*, 5:453; Simon, *Papers of Grant*, 6:155.

26. *OR*, ser. 1, vol. 17, pt. 1, p. 159; Cozzens, *Darkest Days*, 316.

Chapter Six

First Attempts
to Take Vicksburg

Having allowed Earl Van Dorn to escape, U. S. Grant considered his next options. Irritated by Henry Halleck's tendency to leave campaign plans to generals in the field, he bluntly wrote the commanding general, "You have never suggested to me any plan of operations in this department, and as I do not know anything of those [plans] of commanders to my right or left I have none therefore that is not independent of all other forces than those under my immediate command." Grant's words were more than a complaint about the absence of direction from Washington; he clearly wanted greater power to direct operations beyond his own department. He had watched his forces dwindle to shore up the Federal presence in central Tennessee, and he sought leverage to protect his department from future manpower raids. Hoping to gain more attention from Halleck, he pondered taking the offensive, as at Iuka. Perhaps he could persuade Halleck to send troops rather than take them away.[1]

Grant suggested a concentration of Union forces around Grand Junction, Tennessee, for an invasion through northern Mississippi down the track of the Mississippi Central Railroad. That line penetrated all the way to Jackson, the state capital, though it changed names at Canton, north of Jackson, to the New Orleans, Galveston, & Great Northern. Taking Jackson might force the Confederates to evacuate Vicksburg, for the one railroad that ran to Vicksburg—connecting it with Jackson, Meridian, and points east—was the Southern of Mississippi. With this major supply route cut, the Rebel hold on the river city would be tenuous at best. Grant also believed that such an operation would draw Confederate attention away from the Yazoo River, which ran into the Mississippi Delta from just above Vicksburg and supposedly harbored many Rebel vessels that Union army and navy operations needed to destroy. Without those boats the Confederates would have difficulty in bringing supplies from the Delta to Vicksburg. In a thinly disguised effort to get more men, Grant hedged a bit, arguing that he could not undertake such an offensive with the forces he had on hand. His strategy worked quite well. Halleck immediately began seeking reinforcements from the Midwest, and soon thousands of troops were being ordered to the Corinth-Memphis corridor. Halleck also tried to pry men from Samuel Curtis's command in Arkansas.[2]

While Grant maneuvered to build his army and boost his career, one of his former generals, John McClernand, conspired to take the Mississippi Valley campaign, specifically the effort to capture Vicksburg, out of Grant's hands. Since their early days at Belmont and the triumph at Donelson, the Grant-McClernand relationship had deteriorated. McClernand's boastful nature and his annoying tendency to give his troops credit to the disparagement of others grated on Grant's patience. In August 1862, McClernand managed to get leave to return to Illinois and assist in the raising and training of troops. He did that and much more: he used his political connections to get approval from Secretary of War Edwin Stanton and President Lincoln to put together a task force for a downriver expedition to clear the Mississippi all the way to New Orleans, which would mean taking Vicksburg in the process.

McClernand received promises of cooperation from the navy, specifically David Dixon Porter and his flotilla, and also demanded some of the battle-tested veterans of the Army of the Tennessee—Grant's men. McClernand had, after all, been a part of that army and doubtless felt he deserved assistance from its ranks. Yet, however hopeful he may have been about this gambit, the outlook was not as rosy as he thought. His orders from Washington were filled with caveats about Grant's needs possibly taking precedence in decisions regarding the use of Union forces on the Mississippi. Moreover, McClernand's troops would be subject to Halleck's orders and be "employed according to such exigencies as the service in his judgment may require."[3]

Grant, meanwhile, unaware of the attempted intrigue by his former subordinate, continued planning his invasion. He shared with his confidant, William T. Sherman, then commanding in Memphis, his plans for an initial push down the Mississippi Central Railroad beyond Holly Springs. If all went well, Sherman would then lead a contingent of troops from Memphis along the Mississippi & Tennessee Railroad, which ran southeast to Grenada, Mississippi, where it joined the Mississippi Central. The two-pronged

VICKSBURG THEATER
November 1862–July 1863

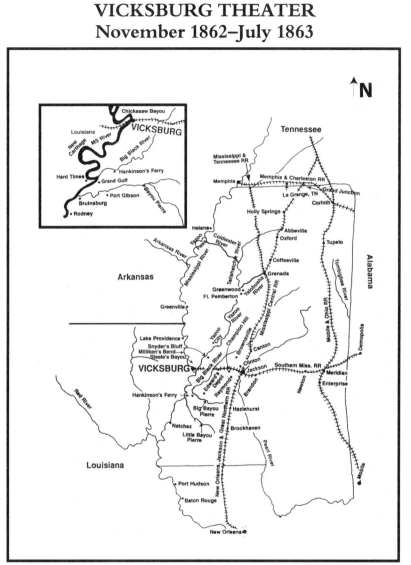

Adapted from Michael B. Ballard, *Pemberton: A Biography* (Jackson: University Press of Mississippi, 1991), 126.

offensive should dilute Rebel strength and force the Confederates to fight or retreat. Grant began concentrating his forces around Grand Junction on November 3. Though he kept Halleck informed, the general in chief remained quiet, tacitly allowing Grant to make plans without interruptions from Washington.[4]

As Grant's divisions gathered in early November, he received scouting reports that the Confederate army, now commanded by John C. Pemberton, had already shown signs of retreating south. Five Union divisions, formed into two wings, marched toward Grand Junction. James McPherson commanded the two divisions on the right wing, and Charles Hamilton the three on the left, some 31,000 men in all. Feeling he still did not have sufficient numbers to go after Pemberton, Grant asked Halleck for an additional seven regiments for himself and sixteen more for Sherman. Despite his decision to become the aggressor, Grant continued to call for more and more troops, clearly indicating that he was nervous about taking the plunge into Mississippi; the Shiloh shadow persisted in tempering his resolve.[5]

Actually, Grant had several good reasons to be tentative, though none had anything to do with his troop strength, which at 31,000 was already greater than Pemberton's. Mississippi's unpredictable winter weather ranged from freezing cold to moderate temperatures, from dry days to extremely rainy periods. The state's roads were generally poor, and a retreating Rebel army would destroy bridges. There would be rivers to cross, and where rivers flowed, wet and perhaps flooded ravines and swamps were sure to be close by. The region was not heavily populated, many people having already moved east to get out of harm's way. The Confederates had foraged over much of the area, negating any notion that Grant's army could live off the land if required.

Finally, the more miles Grant penetrated into Mississippi, the more fragile his lines of supply and communications became. He could, and would, drop off detachments to guard supply depots and to chase away Rebel cavalry trying to cut telegraph and rail lines. Yet problems would be plentiful and the potential great for all sorts of disasters. Grant's determination to stay active led him to make the unwise decision to proceed into northern Mississippi despite the limitations on his supply line. He later claimed that supplies found (that is, foraged from locals) along the Mississippi-Tennessee line proved the fallacy of tying an army to a supply base, yet he overstated the plausibility of living off the land, and in those cases where he claimed to do so, he always kept supply wagons rolling. Any area and its people could do only so much to feed two opposing armies.[6]

Intelligence reports indicated to Grant that he indeed outnumbered Pemberton and encouraged him to boast to Sherman that

Union forces should be able to handle the Rebels "without gloves." To Halleck, he remarked confidently, "I have not the slightest apprehension of a reverse from present appearances"—the same kind of attitude he had displayed before Shiloh. Grant continued to send out scouts and ordered a reconnaissance in force to Holly Springs, which met little enemy resistance. So far, all signs portended success.[7]

Why the change in Grant's attitude? At this point in the war, he seemed to be somewhere between the pre-Shiloh confident general and the post-Shiloh depressed officer devoid of confidence. Iuka and Corinth had brought him praise from Washington and boosted his spirits, yet he had exercised uncharacteristic caution during his preparations for invading Mississippi. On the one hand, he seemed to be again the determined, aggressive, confident Grant; on the other, he appeared reluctant to move on until he was sure that he had enough troops and resources to win—but he did not seem sure just how many or how much would be enough.

At about this time, Grant got word of McClernand's attempts to put together a force to take Vicksburg. The perturbed general fired off a telegram to Halleck: "Am I to understand that I [should] lay here while an Expedition is fitted out from Memphis or do you want me to push as far South as possible? Am I to have Sherman move subject to my order or is he & his forces reserved for some special service? Will not more forces be sent here?" Halleck at once reassured him: "You have command of all troops sent to your department, and have permission to fight the enemy where you please." That news no doubt encouraged Grant, but it also spurred him to rush ahead ill advisedly with his plan to push down the Mississippi Central. He wanted to succeed before McClernand's arrival complicated matters.[8]

Other problems harassed the commanding general as he tried to get his offensive under way. Reports of sporadic vandalism by Union troops always upset him; he tried to walk a fine line between allowing his men to prey upon the property of Rebel sympathizers and taking care not to offend locals loyal to the Union. The problem continued to be discerning who was who, and most of the Union army did not care about the difference. Grant ordered the arrest of arsonists and thieves from time to time, but the issue never went away. The presence of Confederate guerrillas who occasionally ambushed Union troops and Confederate soldiers who did their share of looting exacerbated the situation. Federal soldiers often lashed out at civilians in response to guerrilla attacks, and locals sometimes blamed the Yankees for Rebel depredations. On November 7, 1862, Grant issued Special Field Order No. 1 to warn his officers that unauthorized destruction of civilian property by their men would be charged against them personally: they must control their soldiers or suffer the consequences. He worried about making enemies of area citizens who, if not pro-Union, were not necessarily pro-Confederate, either. At this point in the war he wanted to employ sword and olive branch equally, but the task proved difficult at best.[9]

While Grant struggled with concerns about McClernand and his own undisciplined troops, Samuel Curtis, commanding the Department of the Missouri, suggested to Halleck that a force be sent from Helena, Arkansas, into Pemberton's rear. A fast-moving contingent could destroy railroads behind the Rebels, thereby threatening the enemy supply line. Grant supported the idea, and General A. P. Hovey was assigned to put together the expedition. Meanwhile, Grant asked James McPherson to do additional probing in the Holly Springs area. Grant preferred to draw Pemberton into a decisive battle there if he could, rather than having to pursue the enemy south. McPherson found Rebel troops at the Coldwater River where the Mississippi Central crossed the stream a few miles north of Holly Springs. They did not seem numerous, but Grant feared testing them before more men arrived. No matter how many men Halleck sent, Grant refused to believe he had enough. Despite the pressure of McClernand's activities and the need to beat the Confederates before they retreated deeply into Mississippi, Grant kept insisting that he did not have sufficient strength to overwhelm the enemy.[10]

His hesitation no doubt reflected ever present fears that he might choose the wrong plan, take the wrong road, and wind up in trouble with Washington again. Pondering maps of the region, Grant reviewed varying strategic possibilities. The options he juggled included the already discussed plan of sending Sherman against Pemberton's left. Alternatively, he could order Sherman to Moscow, Tennessee, where his troops would join the rest of the army in one mass moving directly south. Although Grant assured Sherman that the army could live off the countryside and give receipts to citizens from whom goods were taken, he arranged for 600 supply wagons to follow the troops into Mississippi, and trains from the north to bring additional provisions to the front. The army could use food and forage from the area to supplement the supply line, but Grant could not and did not depend on such resources to keep his army going.[11]

On November 14, Grant adopted the plan of sending Sherman from Memphis southeast to Grenada against Pemberton's left. When Sherman marched, Grant would lead the rest of the army south from LaGrange down the Mississippi Central. The two wings would join up either at Holly Springs or possibly farther south at Oxford. Depending upon timing, Sherman might also reinforce the Helena expedition, which was about to proceed. The movement did not begin until the twenty-sixth, and Grant informed Halleck that the offensive had begun. A reluctant Halleck, perhaps concerned about Grant's supply line, responded, "Do not go too far." Grant's wing of the army reached Holly Springs unimpeded, and, accompanied by Julia, he set up headquarters in local homes and watched approvingly as trains brought an abundance of supplies to the Holly Springs depot.[12]

Meanwhile, Hovey's Helena contingent penetrated into Mississippi, his cavalry reaching the railroad northwest of Grenada. After tearing up track and bridges along the Mississippi and Tennessee, however, the Federals retreated, harassed along the way by Confederate riders and infantry detachments sent to chase away the Yankees. Eventually, though Hovey's force escaped with relatively few casualties and the campaign got Pemberton's attention, it accomplished little else, and its ramifications actually hurt Grant's efforts to force a decisive battle. The damage to the railroad was quickly repaired and bridges rebuilt, but the threat to his left convinced Pemberton to retreat farther south. Grant's embrace of diversion and flanking tactics had once more worked; he had forced a significant withdrawal by the enemy. That was the good news. But forcing the Confederates deeper into Mississippi extended Grant's supply and communications lines. In the long view, the raid eliminated the possibility of a quick end to the campaign.[13]

As Sherman and Grant moved forward, word continued to reach Grant's headquarters about McClernand's attempts to take an expedition down the Mississippi River to Vicksburg. Grant became more and more worried, despite the reassurances he had received from Halleck. Fearing of getting bogged down in northern Mississippi led Grant to send Sherman back to Memphis to mount an operation downriver against Vicksburg before McClernand arrived. Pemberton showed no signs of standing and fighting; in fact,

as December dawned, the Confederate general, ever worried about
being flanked—as the Helena expedition in his mind had come too
close to accomplishing—ordered his army to pull south as far as
Grenada. Grant realized that the longer he took to bring the Confederates to bay, the more time McClernand would have to move
downriver and perhaps take Vicksburg. Grant, growing daily more
furious about McClernand's actions, much preferred his friend
Sherman to be in command of river operations. He had grown to
trust Sherman implicitly, always remembering how well Sherman
had fought at Shiloh and, more to the point, how he had stood by
Grant afterward. Since sending Sherman downriver created some
of the same communications problems that had been evident during the Iuka operation, Grant's attitude toward Sherman clearly
stood in stark contrast to his feelings about Rosecrans, who eventually was transferred to Tennessee to command the Army of the
Cumberland.[14]

Meanwhile, to get Washington's approval and to create a buffer
against possible problems in Mississippi for which he might be
blamed, Grant asked Halleck to dictate how far south the army
should pursue Pemberton. Grant did not think he could safely go
farther than Grenada without leaving his supply and communication lines totally vulnerable to Rebel attacks. Would it not be wise
to hold Pemberton in position while Sherman led a force downriver
to hit undermanned Vicksburg? Halleck agreed and, predictably,
gave Grant enough leeway to change plans as circumstances dictated. If Pemberton should abandon Grenada, then Grant should
rethink the Vicksburg operation, for the Confederates might rush
reinforcements to Vicksburg and tear up track to slow Grant's pursuit, thereby leaving Sherman alone to face a formidable force.[15]

On December 8, Grant issued orders authorizing Sherman to
gather an army, including available troops at Helena, for transport
down the Mississippi to assault Vicksburg. Grant, meanwhile, maintained the northern Mississippi front, ever looking for an opening
to force Pemberton into further retreat and allow Union forces to
continue south. While Sherman struggled to gather troops, Grant
tightened his lines and discipline. He ordered the women and children in his family to be sent north to Holly Springs, away from the
army's front at Oxford. He worried over reports that Rebel cavalry,
including skilled horsemen led by the troublesome Nathan Bedford
Forrest, were riding unfettered in West Tennessee, which meant they
could seriously damage the railroad line running north. In response,

Grant sent a portion of his cavalry to watch the railroad junction at Corinth and asked Admiral Porter for assistance should Forrest attempt to cross the Tennessee and cut the railroad.

It was at this time that an irritated Grant issued his infamous order to stop illegal trading activities between Northerners and Confederate sympathizers within his department. He referred to Jews as "a curse to the army," words that caused Abraham Lincoln to revoke the order, which would have expelled "an entire religious class, some of whom are fighting in our ranks." Grant's misstep demonstrated how anxious he had become in trying to make headway toward Vicksburg, protect his supply line, and fend off the ambitions of McClernand.[16] At the same time, Grant set up a remarkable welfare system in northern Mississippi. Still concerned about the negative impact of the war on noncombatants, he decided, "At each post one or more loyal persons will be authorized to keep for sale provisions and absolute necessaries for family use." Those who were in need and able to buy could do so by getting permits, but a fund could be created at the various posts in Grant's department "to supply the necessaries of destitute families gratis," either by levying contributions from disloyal locals able to give or by taxing cotton (taxes to be collected by officers at each post) or "in any other equitable way." Separate accounts would be kept and examined weekly to prevent fraud. Grant continued to hope that the velvet glove approach would build local support for the Union.[17]

While thus occupied, Grant also demonstrated that he had honed his military political skills. McClernand continued to press Washington for a straight answer about his command authority over the river expedition, and Washington—Edwin Stanton in particular—continued to engage in elusive doubletalk. Finally, Stanton told McClernand that he could command a corps but would be under Grant's authority, since Grant commanded the department where McClernand wished to campaign. Grant, upon being so informed, wired orders on December 18, which, as Stanton had instructed, gave McClernand a corps, while Sherman would command another corps. Grant said he hoped McClernand would arrive soon, for "there should be no delay in starting," but McClernand must present a "field return of your entire command—that is, of the river expedition—before starting." Grant well knew that Sherman's expedition would be on its way before McClernand could get to Memphis or take care of the required paperwork. As he wrote later in his memoirs, "I doubted McClernand's fitness; and I had good reason to believe that in forestalling him I was by no means giving offence to those whose authority to command was above both him and me."[18]

Relieved over the successful thwarting of McClernand's interference, Grant continued to solidify his position on the Oxford line. In mid-December he sent a cavalry expedition to raid the Mobile & Ohio Railroad in eastern Mississippi. The Federal riders destroyed about 34 miles of track, captured some 150 prisoners, and caused much consternation in Confederate command circles. On their return to Union lines, the horsemen encountered a large contingent of Confederate cavalry that seemed to be moving north. A mix-up in orders kept this news from Grant for several hours, and by the time he learned of it, a disaster had occurred in his rear at Holly Springs.[19]

On December 20, Earl Van Dorn led a deadly Confederate cavalry assault against Grant's Holly Springs supply base. The Rebel riders overwhelmed surprised Federal defenders and wrecked the depot, causing, in Van Dorn's estimation, some $1.2 million in damages. Livid, Grant ordered pursuit, but Van Dorn led his men into Tennessee and then back into Mississippi, where they eventually made it to the safety of Confederate lines at Grenada. While Van Dorn savaged Holly Springs, Bedford Forrest and his troopers wrecked the Federals' extended supply line farther north in West Tennessee, leaving Grant no choice but to countermarch his columns back to the Corinth-Memphis line. Since the area could not feed his army he had to cut rations until the supply line could be repaired.

The Holly Springs disaster also allowed Pemberton to send reinforcements to Vicksburg to repulse Sherman, who attacked north of the city along Chickasaw Bayou from December 27 to 29, suffered heavy losses, and then pulled back to the Mississippi north of Vicksburg. By then, McClernand had arrived to take over the expedition by virtue of his seniority over Sherman. The two commanders, with David Porter's help, took away some of the sting of Sherman's loss by capturing Arkansas Post, a Confederate stronghold on the Arkansas River. Grant called it a wild goose chase but changed his mind when he later learned that Sherman had endorsed the operation.

An embarrassed Grant now had to pick up the pieces of his first attempt to take Vicksburg. Once more underestimating his opponent, he had lengthened his supply line to the point that it could not be secured, and it proved too tempting for the Confederates to

William T. Sherman. From the National Archives.

pass up. Pemberton had accepted the challenge, and Van Dorn had executed a spectacular raid. Grant wired Sherman of the disaster, and though Sherman received the news before attacking at Chickasaw Bayou, he had gone ahead with his plans and assaulted a well-entrenched enemy protected by difficult, swampy terrain, thus compounding the failed operation in northern Mississippi.

Grant did not give up. His old tenacity came to the fore, and his failures seemed to inspire him now rather than drag him down, as Shiloh had done. Ironically, the McClernand experience taught him that Washington authorities still had faith in him and helped him handle the Holly Springs and Chickasaw Bayou disasters. As 1862 ended, however, Grant could be certain of nothing. Not even the victory at Arkansas Post early in the New Year guaranteed him job security. He must have wondered whether he would be reprimanded or even replaced.

Several factors kept that from happening, and Grant was astute enough to understand most, if not all, of them. Newspaperman Charles Dana, a close friend of Stanton and a future assistant secretary of war, had come to Grant's department allegedly as an observer, but his true role was transparent: he was to check on river operations and deliver intelligence reports to Stanton on the fitness of commanders and their actions. Dana and Grant developed a friendship right away. Certainly, Grant understood the kind of influence, positive or negative, that Dana wielded, so a good, if not close, relationship with Dana was essential, and Grant managed that—though how much the advantageous friendship was based on a natural process of two people liking each other and how much on manipulation by Grant is not known.

Moreover, Grant had won twice back in the fall, at Iuka and Corinth; before Shiloh he had done well; and, after all, he had won at Shiloh. Further, when Grant campaigned, he usually managed to conquer and hold enemy territory. Union lines might be coming south slowly in the West, but they had been advanced much more effectively than those in the East, where the Union Army of the Potomac normally ventured out and then retreated. Grant's overall record was relatively better, whatever his current setbacks. Despite a disappointing December, then, Grant deserved Washington's patience. And it only helped him that John McClernand, early in January 1863, sent a letter to Abraham Lincoln in which he fired volley after volley of accusations against Henry Halleck. Lincoln was not impressed, and surely he and Halleck and Stanton by then understood that Grant, in contrast to McClernand and his angry epistles, was a godsend. Consequently, Grant emerged from December shadows unscathed.[20]

The general thus felt much better than one might have supposed under the circumstances. The ax he had imagined hanging over his head since Shiloh seemed to have disappeared. But he knew he could not relax, for he periodically received prods from Washington about the importance of freeing the Mississippi of Rebels; he must try, and try again, and keep at it until the lower river was clear of Rebel interference. Convinced that he could not trust McClernand—who was disliked by both Sherman and Porter as well as by other officers who did not take to his overbearing style—to do anything worthwhile on the river, Grant knew he must remedy the command situation. Despite his personal feelings, he hesitated to give Sherman authority over McClernand, since the latter outranked the former. Therefore, to avoid any outcry that might follow such a decision, Grant decided to go downriver and take personal command of operations on the Mississippi.

NOTES

1. *OR*, ser. 1, vol. 17, pt. 2, p. 296; Grant, *Memoirs*, 281; Edwin C. Bearss, *The Vicksburg Campaign*, 3 vols. (Dayton, OH, 1985–1986), 1:21.

2. *OR*, ser. 1, vol. 17, pt. 2, pp. 296, 308; Simpson, *Grant*, 155; Bearss, *Vicksburg*, 1:23.

3. Richard L. Kiper, *Major General John Alexander McClernand: Politician in Uniform* (Kent, OH, 1999), 129–43; *OR*, ser. 1, vol. 17, pt. 2, pp. 174–75, 282.

4. *OR*, ser. 1, vol. 17, pt. 2, pp. 312–13, 315–19.

5. Ibid., pp. 338–40; Simon, *Papers of Grant*, 6:243, 256, 261.

6. Grant, *Memoirs*, 289–91.

7. Simon, *Papers of Grant*, 6:262–63, 268, 278.

8. Ibid., 6:288; *OR*, ser. 1, vol. 17, pt. 1, p. 469.

9. *OR*, ser. 1, vol. 17, pt. 2, pp. 326–27; Simon, *Papers of Grant*, 6:266–67.

10. *OR*, ser. 1, vol. 13, pp. 778–79; vol. 17, pt. 2, pp. 322–24, 328, 331.

11. Ibid., vol. 17, pt. 2, pp. 336, 348.

12. Ibid., p. 348; pt. 1, p. 471.

13. Ibid., pt. 1, pp. 528–41.

14. Ibid., pt. 2, pp. 396, 408, 412; Grant, *Memoirs*, 288; Simpson, *Grant*, 166.

15. *OR*, ser. 1, vol. 17, pt. 1, pp. 472–73.

16. Ibid., pt. 2, pp. 376, 400, 404, 415, 424; Simon, *Papers of Grant*, 7:54.

17. *OR*, ser. 1, vol. 17, pt. 2, p. 405.

18. Ibid., pp. 420, 425; Grant, *Memoirs*, 288.

19. *OR*, ser. 1, vol. 17, pt. 2, pp. 438–39; pt. 1, pp. 496–99.

20. Basler, *Lincoln*, 6:70–71; McFeely, *Grant*, 120–21; Simpson, *Grant*, 155.

Chapter Seven

Months of Frustration

Before leaving Memphis, Grant ordered detachments to repair rail lines and otherwise restore some normalcy following the Van Dorn–Forrest raids. He also instructed his officers to make sure pro-Confederate families in northern Mississippi west of Corinth were forced out, and he wanted to expel openly rebellious Memphis citizens as well. Their activities had progressed beyond verbal protestations to espionage and destruction, and Grant had had enough. Though anxious about getting additional troops downriver, he wanted to keep the Memphis-Corinth corridor, and West Tennessee in general, stabilized to deter Confederate cavalry and guerrilla raids. In addition, news from Tennessee that Rosecrans had forced Bragg to withdraw after a two-day contest at Murfreesboro, Tennessee, obligated Grant to keep a wary eye on what Bragg's next move might be.[1]

Fortunately, military activities settled down and immediate dangers dissipated, allowing Grant to return his attention to river operations. He held meetings with Sherman, McClernand, and Porter and decided to keep the army busy while he studied maps and planned for renewed efforts to take Vicksburg. He recalled, "The water was very high and the rains were incessant. There seemed no possibility of a land movement before the end of March or later, and it would not do to lie idle all this time." Grant feared negative effects on health and, both among his troops and in the North, on morale. Since the problem before him was "how to secure a landing on high ground east of the Mississippi without an apparent retreat," he began what he termed "a series of experiments to consume time, and to divert the attention of the enemy, of my troops and of the public generally. I myself, never felt great confidence that any of the experiments resorted to would prove successful. Nevertheless I was always prepared to take advantage of them in case they did."[2]

Grant no doubt understood that many of his soldiers had tired of the long campaigning that so far had not produced major advances.

Conditions along river lowlands on the Louisiana side of the Mississippi were especially unhealthy, and frequent flooding made camp life extremely miserable. Abraham Lincoln's Emancipation Proclamation of January 1, 1863, did not sit well with many in Grant's army, who believed they were fighting to restore the Union rather than to free the slaves. Though the numbers are undocumented, soldiers' letters reveal that many of their comrades deserted. They must have been a minority, however, because neither then nor later did Grant express concern. The majority apparently maintained a trust in their fellow midwesterner, who seemed determined to win. Despite his ups and downs, they sensed in Grant an admirable steadfastness. As long as he did not quit, neither would they.

The first "experiment" involved revitalizing a former project that had failed: Grant decided to try again the building of a canal across the neck of land opposite Vicksburg in the same area as one that had been abandoned in the summer of 1862 during naval operations against the city. At that time, infantry under the command of Thomas Williams had tried to divert the course of the Mississippi away from Vicksburg, but engineering problems and weather combined to doom the effort. After looking the place over and conferring with his engineers, Grant decided that the first canal location had been poorly chosen. If the troops dug a new canal above the original ditch, the river current should hit it with enough velocity to cut through the new channel and divert the Mississippi. If anything could be accomplished around Vicksburg in the early winter months of 1863, it would have to be done on the peninsula, for the lowlands north of the city, where Sherman's attacks had failed, were flooded.[3]

Grant did some arm-twisting too, while he waited for feedback from Washington on the canal idea. Again reminding Halleck that his authority was limited by the confines of departmental boundaries, Grant renewed his argument that having control over a broad span of western departments would permit a commander to maneuver troops more quickly and effectively. Grant did not openly ask for such a combined command for himself; in fact, he said he would prefer staying where he was. Still, he envisioned having more power, if only to deal better with scheming officers such as McClernand. He had enough trouble just managing his own responsibilities without having to worry about other officers maneuvering to undercut his authority.[4]

Grant received a welcome boost to his confidence when he learned that President Lincoln endorsed a larger command area, and he was given authority over all the Union troops in Arkansas that he needed to pursue operations on the Mississippi. Halleck assigned Willis Gorman's command to McClernand's XIII Corps, though Gorman continued for the moment his campaign to clear the Arkansas and White Rivers of Rebel vessels. Grant notified McClernand of Gorman's assignment and told him that shovels for the canal project were on the way. He also asked for any news from Nathaniel Banks, then downriver around Baton Rouge, but Banks remained tied down in Louisiana and never assisted the Vicksburg campaign. Grant had to depend on Halleck to keep funneling more troops downriver from the Midwest.[5]

Grant stayed in Memphis longer than he planned, not leaving for good until January 26. While there, he continued efforts to elimi-nate the headaches that Southern sympathizers caused in the city, saying at one point that if necessary he would not oppose driving men, women, and children into exile if it would do any good. Fi-nally, he decided to leave the matter in Stephen Hurlbut's hands; Hurlbut had a hard streak that would help keep the lid on guer-rilla activity around Memphis. Grant was concerned, too, about the paucity of information from downriver, though continuing rains made it obvious that there had likely been no progress worth reporting.

Since Grant had brought up the matter of the canal, official Wash-ington wanted to know how the project was going. President Lin-coln, ever anxious for news of real progress in the war, "attache[d] much importance to this," according to Halleck. After Grant ar-rived at Young's Point above Vicksburg, he reviewed reports and concluded that the canal was not likely to work anytime soon. Progress seemed so uncertain that Grant considered other options, such as cutting the levee upstream below Helena on the east side of the Mississippi at a place called Yazoo Pass. If that idea worked, Union transports and gunboats might be able to enter the pass and descend through the heart of Mississippi via inland rivers to a point north of Vicksburg on the Yazoo River. He carefully reviewed this and additional methods of bypassing the Vicksburg batteries. Wa-terways on the west side of the Mississippi via Lake Providence, above Vicksburg, leading south to where the Red River emptied into the Mississippi, offered possibilities of getting the Union army beyond the Confederate batteries for a landing below Vicksburg.

John A. McClernand. From the National Archives.

In the midst of examining operational pros and cons, Grant suddenly found himself once more having to deal with the ever present troublemaker. McClernand, either out of conviction or just to be annoying, was acting as if he were in command of the river expedition, though Stanton and Halleck had made it clear that he was not. He berated Grant for sending messages directly to corps commanders rather than funneling them through his headquarters,

saying, quite rightly, "Two generals cannot command this army."
Grant, of course, called McClernand's bluff, and, with remarkable
patience, reminded him that when he, Grant, took direct command
of river operations, McClernand had been assigned to head the XIII
Corps and had no powers beyond that corps. Grant did not need
McClernand to tell him that Lincoln was commander in chief; accordingly, he agreed to accept whatever directives might come from
the White House. Previously told by Halleck that he had command
of all forces in his district, Grant was not surprised, and undoubtedly smiled, when McClernand's protestations fell on deaf ears in
Washington.[6]

Despite recent debacles and administrative headaches, Grant's
confidence level continued to rise. In this case, unlike the aftermath of Shiloh, Grant had escaped either the wrath of a superior
officer or the heavy censure of public opinion. The Washington leadership, including his former nemesis Halleck, liked Grant's overall
record, his quiet resolve, and his determination, and their support
in turn gave Grant self-assurance that he had not felt in some time.
With it came a commitment to persist, no matter what obstacles
might appear, including the troublesome McClernand. The Mississippi must be cleared, meaning that Vicksburg must be taken, so
Grant focused on accomplishing that goal, whatever the frustrations and setbacks—and there would soon be more of both. At the
right moment, however, he had gotten what he needed: the support of Halleck, Stanton, and Lincoln. He no longer wasted valuable time wringing his hands over a McClernand-like threat.

The immediate frustration that taxed Grant's grit continued to
be the canal. Despite a massive effort by thousands of Union soldiers, the project got bogged down in high water and heavy rains.
Nature seemed intent on dooming this second attempt to bypass
Vicksburg's river batteries. The lowlands on the Louisiana side became one gigantic quagmire, and soldiers armed with shovels lived
a miserable existence, fighting floods and mud and occasionally
dodging Rebel cannon shot. Grant and his engineers soon realized
that they had miscalculated in the same manner as those who had
failed in the summer of 1862. By early February, nothing had
changed; the Mississippi flowed by the opening as if it were not
there.

Mindful that the eyes of the president, Halleck, and Stanton
were on him, Grant sent optimistic reports to Washington, but it
would take more than a positive attitude to rescue the canal. The

intensive work continued through February and into March, and
dredges were set up which, along with better weather, improved
the outlook for success. But fluctuating water levels and Confederate gunners still thwarted the work, and by late March, Grant accepted the inevitable and gave up the whole effort.[7]

He had not counted on the canal alone, however; several other
projects continued. One involved Lake Providence, a crescent-
shaped body of water some 75 river miles above Vicksburg on the
Louisiana side of the river. Union engineers believed that with
proper cutting of levees, lowland waterways could be used by vessels entering Lake Providence to travel all the way to the Red River.
If the plan worked, Grant could guarantee the navy and transports
safe passage past Vicksburg and land his army in Mississippi below Vicksburg, without the risk of passing by the Confederate cannon on the city's high ground bordering the river. Grant assigned
engineer James McPherson to head up the effort.[8]

Even before McPherson took steps to get the project under way,
Grant had second thoughts. The waterway connections, usually
small channels washed out by floods, were so full of trees and their
water levels varied so greatly that moving loaded troop transports
safely through these streams seemed highly problematic.
McPherson remained convinced that he could succeed and even
make it possible for heavy naval vessels to steam all the way to the
Red; Grant, however, was just as certain that it had been a bad idea.
With his impatience growing daily, he allowed McPherson to continue, but he himself focused on other possibilities, in part because
he had become quite restless but, more to the point, he needed some
breakthrough to keep official Washington on his side and convinced
that he was making progress to clear the Mississippi. He had been
around long enough now to understand that keeping his job depended more on current achievement than on past performance.
He must keep pushing ahead with whatever tactics seemed
promising.[9]

Grant preferred continuing innovative approaches to meet the
challenge of taking Vicksburg. The failed overland attempt down
the Mississippi Central was fresh on his mind, and, despite urgings
from Sherman, he had no desire to go back and try that again. For
to pull away from Vicksburg and the river now and return to the
Memphis-Corinth front would appear to be a retreat, and neither
Washington nor public opinion nor Grant himself would stand for
that.

One possibility that had captured Grant's imagination weeks earlier, and to which he kept returning, was the Yazoo Pass gambit. It seemed all the more plausible because, according to his engineers, explosives could blast a passageway to the pass from the Mississippi; boats could enter the pass into a lake and then negotiate one narrow connecting channel to the Coldwater River. From that point on, the inland rivers would rise, thanks to water flowing in from the Mississippi via the pass, and provide easy routes south. Grant needed the cooperation of David Porter, and Porter seemed amenable to doing whatever Grant and Sherman wanted, despite his innate dislike of West Pointers. The three men liked one another, and they had a common antagonist in McClernand, whose arrogance Porter had come to detest during the Arkansas Post campaign. Grant knew, too, that any success would depend on naval assistance.

Yazoo Pass was a tiny bayou on the Mississippi side of the Mississippi River, located a few miles below Helena, Arkansas. If naval transports filled with infantry, along with Porter's gunboats, could get through a breach in the levee and into the Coldwater River, they could follow it south to the Tallahatchie, which joined with the Yalobusha at Greenwood, Mississippi, to form the Yazoo River. The Yazoo descended southwest to the bluffs north of Vicksburg. If boats could take troops to the bluffs, the Union army would have a foothold from which to attack the city. Troops on the high ground would have advantages that Sherman's had not had when they attacked across Chickasaw Bayou against Rebels holding the hills.

The risks were obvious: the Rebels were not likely to sit idly by and let this all happen without throwing up some kind of resistance. Yet Grant believed the plan would work. The Delta region traversed by the key rivers was already flooded in places from winter rains and from the absence of sufficient levees, and cutting the levee for access to Yazoo Pass would raise water levels. High water should make passage easy for Union boats, even loaded transports and heavy ironclads. The supply line would be long, but several of the plantations that dotted the landscape along the rivers had some dry ground; perhaps food could be found at those places until supply boats could follow the main force as it snaked south. It was a long route, which meant that many things could go wrong, just as they had in northern Mississippi in December. Grant considered all these possibilities and told his engineers to proceed. The Yazoo Pass project soon got under way.

Although there were many delays in getting into the Coldwater because of trees choking the narrow access waterway, the expedition began moving south. Until it was near Greenwood, the transports, troops, and ironclads had a rather uneventful trip downstream. But while descending the Tallahatchie, vessels leading the way spotted a Rebel obstruction in the distance: the Confederates had constructed a fort, named Pemberton in honor of the departmental commander, near Greenwood, along the north bank of a neck of land where the Tallahatchie abruptly turned east before it met the Yalobusha to form the Yazoo. Fort Pemberton proved to be a tough obstacle; Union troops could do little to flank the Confederate position because of flooded countryside on either side of the Tallahatchie channel. The campaign quickly bogged down to exchanges of artillery and small arms fire, resulting in a stalemate that showed no signs of a breakthrough by either army. Grant, reading reports from the expedition, concluded that his optimism had been misguided; this latest adventure would go no farther than Greenwood.[10]

While his troops wasted time in front of Fort Pemberton, Grant listened to David Porter's proposal for another way to gain a foothold on the bluffs north of Vicksburg. Porter wanted to take a flotilla from the Mississippi up into the Yazoo—the old Chickasaw Bayou approach—and turn into Steele's Bayou. From that stream the boats would go into Black Bayou, Deer Creek, the Rolling Fork, and the Big Sunflower, which emptied into the Yazoo above the fortified bluffs north of Vicksburg and south of Yazoo City. If everything went well, Porter could then turn north and force the Confederates to abandon Fort Pemberton, thus allowing the stalled Yazoo Pass expedition to come on down the Yazoo.

Grant liked the prospects enough to go with Porter on a tour of the first leg of the journey. After seeing the low-hanging limbs of towering trees obstructing parts of Steele's Bayou, Grant wondered just how well Porter's five cumbersome ironclads would negotiate the twists and turns they were sure to encounter. The Union had already lost one ironclad to a Yazoo River mine planted by the enemy, and Grant did not want any more boats meeting the fate of the USS *Cairo*, which had sunk back in December. He therefore alerted Sherman and McPherson to provide infantry and field artillery support as might be needed by Porter, and the new campaign was on.

David Dixon Porter. From the Robert Younger Collection, Dayton, Ohio. *Courtesy of Robert Younger*

As the ironclads pushed their way along, the flotilla finally made it to Deer Creek, which Sherman and Porter reconnoitered. Sherman was not impressed with the flooded countryside that negated much of the support his troops might provide. He suggested taking Deer Creek directly into the Yazoo, rather than continuing the roundabout route plotted by Porter. The admiral insisted on staying with his original plan, got bogged down by Confederate obstructions, and almost lost his boats before beginning a retrograde movement that, with Sherman's help, managed to elude the Rebels and allow the boats to return safely to the Yazoo. Had the Confederates been more aggressive, Porter might not have been so fortunate.[11]

The Yazoo Pass campaign continued to be a stalemate, with the Confederate defenses at Fort Pemberton growing ever stronger. Grant finally decided to commit no more troops there but allowed his commanders to stay on for a time, just in case some unforeseen opportunity arose to make headway. Grant knew how a return to the Mississippi would look to Lincoln and the War Department. Federal pressure increased on the Confederates holding the fort, but though the standoff passed through various stages, ebbing and flowing briefly in favor of one side or the other, the overall picture did not change. Finally, accepting the obvious, Grant called off the operation in early April.[12]

By this time he had yet another plan in mind, one that ultimately proved successful. It had become obvious to him that he had to get his army south of Vicksburg before he could begin field operations against the city itself. The terrain north of the city, with its swamplands, narrow streams, and towering bluffs, had proved very resistant to both his troops and Porter's boats. Somehow he had to figure a way to move his army past the Vicksburg waterfront batteries and land them on the Mississippi side of the river. The attempts to find ways to the south by routes other than the Mississippi had failed. As March wound down, Grant and his staff came to a decision.

By that time, a beleaguered Grant needed a boost. He had escaped the debacles of Holly Springs and Chickasaw Bayou without retribution from Washington but had subsequently experienced a series of setbacks. Grant later recalled the crux of the situation existing along the Mississippi during those first three frustrating months of 1863:

> This long, dreary and, for heavy and continuous rains and high water, unprecedented winter was one of great hardship to all engaged about Vicksburg. The river was higher than its natural banks from December, 1862, to the following April. The war had suspended peaceful pursuits in the South, further than the pro-

U. S. Grant, 1863. From the author's collection.

duction of army supplies, and in consequence the levees were
neglected and broken in many places and the whole country was
covered with water. Troops could scarcely find dry ground on
which to pitch their tents. Malarial fevers broke out among the
men. Measles and small-pox also attacked them. The hospital ar-
rangements and medical attendance were so perfect, however, that
the loss of life was much less than might have been expected.
Visitors to the camps went home with dismal stories to relate;
Northern papers came back to the soldiers with these stories exaggerated. Because I would not divulge my ultimate plans to visitors, they pronounced me idle, incompetent and unfit to command
men in an emergency, and clamored for my removal.

Clearly, Grant remained sensitive to the burdens of command and to criticism of his generalship.[13]

The outcry progressed to the point that some newspapers offered suggestions for his successor, among them McClernand, which must have particularly infuriated Grant. Yet he determined to persist as long as Halleck, Stanton, and Lincoln supported him, whether the support was vocal or quiet, and their support remained firm, however nervous they may have been at the lack of success on the lower Mississippi. Official Washington was likely more nervous about, and more focused on, the situation in the eastern theater, where the Army of the Potomac was undergoing yet another command change (from Ambrose Burnside to Joseph Hooker). Grant's long distance from the capital and the turmoil in the eastern army certainly deflected attention from the Mississippi Valley.

No one familiar with the facts could accuse Grant of being idle, as were too many other Union commanders. He had kept pressure on the Confederates and made them guess as to his true intentions—which, despite his protestations to the contrary, he likely did not always know himself. Whatever his lack of operational success, Grant's various moves had kept Pemberton off balance and forced the Confederates to scatter their military resources, which were already inferior to those Grant had at his disposal.[14]

With Pemberton at the helm in Mississippi, Grant concluded by the spring of 1863 that he need not fear a Confederate offensive. The Rebel commanders reacted to what he did but did not seem inclined to come after him; except for the brief flash of Van Dorn's raid, they appeared content to stay on the defensive, giving Grant room for experimentation and offensive maneuver that he might not otherwise have had. The January–March period of campaigning had demonstrated that he could plan whatever offensive he pleased. Enemy resistance, helped greatly by the elements and terrain, might throw him back, but such setbacks were temporary. He had more men, more guns, and a navy with which to carry the war to the Confederates. He needed only a combination of the right circumstances that would allow him to proceed.

Those circumstances began to fall into place as the landscape dried out. Grant had been in touch with Halleck about preparations to implement his latest idea: moving the army down the Louisiana side of the Mississippi to a point well south of Vicksburg, where the navy could transport them across to the Mississippi side. The logistics of such a move were mind-boggling. Grant needed hundreds of transports—anything that would float and carry a few hundred men would do—and Halleck did his best to round them up without infuriating other western generals who also needed river support. From Helena north to St. Louis and beyond, men had been congregating for some time, and the transports were needed to get them to Milliken's Bend on the Louisiana side of the Mississippi, whence the march south would begin. Whatever the challenges involved, this plan made much more sense than a direct assault on the Vicksburg bluffs from the river, a return trip to northern Mississippi, or another assault on the bluffs that bordered the Yazoo, all ideas that had been bandied about at Grant's headquarters. The first would be suicidal and the other two would only revive failed strategies. Grant listened to such recommendations, but he kept his mind on getting his army south of Vicksburg.[15]

Grant and his generals rejoiced as "waters began to recede; the roads crossing the peninsula behind the levees of the bayous, were emerging from the waters." The drying-out took time, but there would soon be dry land enough to blaze a trail through the Louisiana lowlands. Engineers had to bridge ditches and streams, and Porter had to move the empty transports past the troublesome but seldom lethal batteries at Vicksburg. David Farragut's operations in the summer of 1862 had proved that Union boats could successfully run the gauntlet of those Rebel guns; now and then their artillery scored a hit, but myriad technical problems, most pertaining to angle of fire and poor location, kept Confederate gunners from turning the riverfront into a no-man's-land. The heavy cannon could not be shifted about to produce converging fire or depressed enough to shoot down at boats hugging the Vicksburg shore. Moreover, Union rifle fire from the Louisiana side of the river made the rate of Rebel fire sporadic. By using proper tactics, then, boats could make it safely by the waterfront. Porter and Grant knew it had been done and could be done again; it would be up to Porter to make it happen.[16]

Although the Rebels still firmly controlled Vicksburg, U. S. Grant believed that at last a turning point had been reached in Union operations. His troops had slogged through the Delta and endured the Louisiana swamplands; their experiences had been dismal, but they had been toughened by it all and now sensed that perhaps the campaign had taken a positive turn. Grant and his men felt a new momentum; he and his lieutenants must keep it going.

Confronting the vastness and nature of the area around Vicksburg had been challenging, but it had given Grant an opportunity to practice his tactics of diversion. In the process, he had forced Pemberton to react defensively, scattering his outnumbered forces. Grant understood now that campaigns of maneuver often produced a superiority of numbers, enhancing potential victory. Despite all the disappointments, he had maintained the initiative, made the enemy uncertain about how to react, and kept Union troops busy and hopeful for success. His attempts to take Vicksburg so far had been characterized by innovation and determination. His next operation would require a great deal of both.

NOTES

1. Simon, *Papers of Grant*, 7:121, 138, 158, 167–68, 189.
2. Grant, *Memoirs*, 296–97.
3. Simon, *Papers of Grant*, 7:233–34, 241–42, 272n.
4. Ibid., 7:234.
5. Ibid., 7:242–43; *OR*, ser. 1, vol. 17, pt. 2, p. 578; vol. 24, pt. 1, p. 9; John D. Winters, *The Civil War in Louisiana* (Baton Rouge, 1963), 174.
6. Simon, *Papers of Grant*, 7:245, 249, 252–54, 264, 267, 306.
7. *OR*, ser. 1, vol. 24, pt. 3, pp. 7, 9, 13, 38, 51–52; pt. 1, p. 18; Grant, *Memoirs*, 298, 303; Sherman, *Memoirs*, 226, 229.
8. *OR*, ser. 1, vol. 24, pt. 3, p. 44; Bearss, *Vicksburg*, 1:470.
9. Grant, *Memoirs*, 298–99, 303; Bearss, *Vicksburg*, 1:473; *OR*, ser. 1, vol. 24, pt. 1, p. 21.
10. Grant, *Memoirs*, 299–301. On the Yazoo Pass campaign see Bearss, *Vicksburg*, 1:479–548.
11. Grant, *Memoirs*, 301–2. On Deer Creek operations see Bearss, *Vicksburg*, 1:549–91.
12. *OR*, ser. 1, vol. 24, pt. 1, p. 151.
13. Grant, *Memoirs*, 304.
14. Ibid.
15. Ibid., 305–7.
16. Ibid., 305–6.

CHAPTER EIGHT

APRIL 1863

U. S. GRANT IMPLIED in later years that throughout the early months of 1863 he had focused solely on getting his army south of Vicksburg. Yet even as he made plans to carry out the maneuver that proved to be the turning point in the Vicksburg campaign, Grant continued to look at other options. Though still confident that he could take Vicksburg, he hedged; as late as March 22 he notified Nathaniel Banks that an assault on Snyder's Bluff north of Vicksburg was still possible. Perhaps Grant held out a measure of hope that the Fort Pemberton expedition might still by some miracle succeed, but he worried about the dispersal of his troops that his many trials and failures had caused. True, he had forced Pemberton to scatter Confederate troops in response; nevertheless, Grant now had to concentrate his army, and that would take time.

Grant's tentativeness, at the very time he claimed to have made a hard, firm decision, demonstrated that ghosts of the past had not completely left him. Just when he appeared to have freed himself of doubts, some of the old uncertainties came back to haunt him. At this point, however, he got a needed jolt from Halleck. Perhaps concerned that Grant might keep trying plans that went nowhere, Halleck pointedly wrote: "The great object on our line now is the opening of the Mississippi River, and everything else must tend to that purpose. The eyes and ears of the whole country are now directed to your army. In my opinion, the opening of the Mississippi River will be to us of more advantage than the capture of forty Richmonds." He added that Grant should concentrate on his plan to bypass Vicksburg and let Banks take care of himself. If Banks could help, fine, but if not, Grant should still push on.[1]

The words remedied Grant's wavering; after all, in the past he had uttered the same sentiments, but the reminder came at a propitious time. Rather than continuing to wonder about other possible strategies, Grant set to work on plans to get his army down the Louisiana side. He chose as a staging area a settlement downriver called New Carthage, about 35 miles south of Milliken's

Bend and beyond range of the Confederate cannon on the southern flank of Vicksburg. On March 29, Grant gave orders for the
march south to begin; John McClernand's corps led the way.[2]

Many historians have ignored the implications of Grant's decision to place McClernand in the lead. Grant was putting his career
on the line: if this move failed, he likely would be removed from
command, regardless of Washington's previous support. So why
did he allow his nemesis to be in the vanguard of the operation?
Part of the answer lies in simple logic. McClernand's corps was
already in the Milliken's Bend area (they had been stationed there
since the Arkansas Post campaign, working on the failed canal
project downriver) and thus required little mobilization to get on
the road to New Carthage. Further, McClernand's position on the
point meant constant communication between him and Grant,
which allowed Grant to keep close tabs on this general he did not
totally trust. More significantly, McClernand liked the plan, whereas
Sherman did not, and McPherson, though promising, was young
and inexperienced. Grant wrote that he decided to travel with
McClernand to make sure his subordinate behaved. He believed,
he said, that McClernand might take credit for the whole thing if it
worked, but even if he did not come right out and say so, Grant
could live with that. The truth seems to be that though he found
McClernand arrogant, presumptuous, and overly opportunistic, he
respected the man's ability to command in the field. For all these
reasons, then, he gave the important advance position to
McClernand, and it would not be the last time in the Vicksburg
campaign that he counted on this political general to get the job
done.

While McClernand and his staff organized the march, Grant
looked to one last canal possibility to facilitate transportation of
other troops and supplies to New Carthage. This plan involved
digging a canal inland on the Louisiana side, north of Vicksburg,
from Duckport Landing to Walnut Bayou, which would in theory
allow flatboats loaded with supplies to travel via inland waterways
to New Carthage. Work was well along when Grant decided that
low water made the scheme unworkable, and like the other attempted bypasses, it died before completion.[3]

Even though he had been told to proceed with or without Banks,
Grant received a note from Washington urging him to cooperate
with Banks if the opportunity arose. Banks had political connections, so the Lincoln administration did not want it to appear that

Grant was ignoring him. Grant responded by telling McClernand that once the army had crossed the river into Mississippi at the port town of Grand Gulf south of Vicksburg, forces should be sent to support Banks's efforts to capture Port Hudson above Baton Rouge. Then Banks's and McClernand's troops could come up to help take Vicksburg. Nothing of the sort ever happened, and it is not clear that Grant ever expected it to, but by issuing the instructions, he had at least humored the War Department.[4]

The march south would not be easy. Confederate cavalry in Louisiana harassed McClernand's advance patrols, but if the move at times seemed ponderous, it was inexorable. Grant occasionally checked with McClernand, and from time to time he grew irritated at the slow pace, but the men kept going, and McPherson's corps prepared to follow.[5]

As the XIII Corps approached New Carthage, Grant and David Porter discussed the navy's role. Porter agreed to help set up the New Carthage base and coordinate the passage of transports past the Vicksburg batteries. Grant made it clear that a couple of ironclads would be needed south of Vicksburg to silence the Rebel big guns there. Porter was willing to comply, but he told Grant that this current operation must be set in stone if ironclads moving downriver were vital parts of the overall plan, for they would likely have to remain downstream for a while. They would not have enough power to come back up against the strong current, and even if they tried, they would be going so slowly that enemy guns might cause problems.

Porter no doubt feared that Grant's somewhat erratic decision-making since the first of the year might continue. In fact, perhaps to appease those who still did not believe the move south would work, Grant agreed to steam up the Yazoo with Sherman and Porter to look at the bluffs. What he saw convinced him that he must listen to no more nonsense about sending men against the impressive enemy works there. He told Porter that the operation south was firm; there would be no turning back.[6]

As Grant hoped and counted on, Pemberton allowed Union forces to move south practically unmolested. Except for occasional pesky Louisiana cavalry, McClernand's troops found no major resistance other than terrain and flood problems. John Bowen, Pemberton's best general and currently commanding at Grand Gulf, south of Vicksburg, received reports about the large Union columns moving down the other side of the river, and he warned Pemberton that something should be done to meet this threat. Pemberton did not think so, but he allowed Bowen to send troops across to check the veracity of scouting reports and chase away any Yankees they found. The sortie accomplished nothing more than to verify intelligence that numerous Federals were on the move, for Bowen did not have enough men to block McClernand.[7]

As the Union army continued marching, Porter prepared for the run past the Vicksburg batteries. One of the most valuable lessons learned from Farragut's 1862 campaign was that the difficult shooting angles caused by the location of the enemy guns put boats close to the Mississippi side of the river in less danger from Confederate cannon than those in the middle or on the Louisiana side. He decided to start out along the Louisiana shore in the dark, hoping that the flotilla might get by the batteries without being noticed; if they should be seen and the Confederates started firing, then the vessels would shift to the Mississippi shoreline. That tactic, plus muffled engine noise, the use of cotton and hay for padding, and barges strapped to boats for protection, all worked in Porter's favor. The spectacular night passing of the batteries on April 16 would long be remembered by those who saw it, but for U. S. Grant it was nerve-wracking. Yet only one boat was lost, and when six days later more came by with minimal losses, he was delighted. The Confederate guns continued to be ineffective against passing vessels, and the arrival of transports below Vicksburg meant that another part of the grand Union design had fallen into place.[8]

Grant knew that the passing of the batteries and the march south might tip off Pemberton as to what was going on, so he set diversionary tactics in motion to keep his opponent guessing. Previous diversions had unnerved the Confederate commander, and Grant did not hesitate to stay with successful strategy. Hence, Frederick Steele took his division to Greenville, Mississippi, upriver from Vicksburg and then inland and back south toward the hill city. Sherman led a diversion up the Yazoo from where it emptied into the Mississippi; he carried it out too tentatively to be very effective, not convincing the Confederates that he was making a real attack. Still, his mere presence held up decisions to send troops south from the city to reinforce Bowen. These developments, plus river traffic headed north resulted from an effort to clear congestion on the Mississippi, all worked to thwart Pemberton's attempts to understand Grant's true intentions. He even convinced himself for a time that Grant had given up and was preparing to return north to Memphis.[9]

John C. Pemberton. From the Library of Congress.

The one diversion that distracted Pemberton more than any other was a spectacular cavalry raid that cut through the heart of Mississippi from the northeastern part of the state to Baton Rouge, Louisiana. Benjamin Grierson led a column of some 1,700 riders out of La Grange, Tennessee, on April 17 and arrived in the Louisiana capital on May 2. Along the way he sent out detachments to tear up railroad track, burn supplies, and generally wreak havoc in the countryside, while staying almost constantly on the move. Grant called it "one of the most brilliant cavalry exploits of the war." Even more, it was one of the most brilliant tactical concepts of the war, and Grant deserved the credit for it.[10]

The myriad operations attempted before April made possible the effectiveness of these current diversions. Grant's efforts to keep his troops in motion, operating in varying directions, had so totally befuddled Pemberton and his commanders that additional diversions enacted to protect the Union army's move south worked even better than they might have otherwise. Looking at the big picture, one can see that Grant had managed to turn the negatives since January 1, 1863, into positives. Certainly he had learned that moving constantly with his superior numbers and keeping his enemy off balance brought him many advantages, so that taking a risk on the Louisiana side of the river turned out to be less chancy than he may have feared.

As Pemberton tried to figure out Grant's intentions and Bowen begged for reinforcements, Grant addressed his next major decision: where his troops should cross the river into Mississippi. After studying maps, Grant settled on occupying Grand Gulf for use as a base on the Mississippi side. Porter, asked to scout the place, found well-fortified heights close to the landing, where Bowen had established two forts. But with both McClernand's and McPherson's corps now crowding into New Carthage, something had to be done to relieve the congestion.

Porter reasoned that the longer Union forces waited to take Grand Gulf, the more formidable the Rebel defenses there were likely to become. Once he saw Bowen's forts, Grant thought Porter had exaggerated their strength. Porter, no doubt remembering his Deer Creek fiasco, rejected as too risky Grant's request to take a detachment of boats above Grand Gulf, into and up the Big Black River, to sever Bowen's supply line. Meanwhile, McClernand pushed on south of New Carthage and found another base at a place called Hard Times. Grant told McClernand to concentrate in that area, opposite Grand Gulf, and to be ready to board transports to cross the river.[11]

Before any crossing could be made, however, the Confederates had to be chased away from Grand Gulf. On April 29, Porter's fleet of seven ironclads assaulted Bowen's position, steaming by the

Confederate works in an oval formation in order to keep up a steady stream of fire. Bowen's gunners answered effectively, and both sides scored telling hits. The Confederates damaged Porter's flagship, causing it to drift ashore; fortunately for Porter and his crew, it stopped in a location that Confederate artillery could not reach. After nearly six hours of stalemate, Grant had seen enough. He sent word to McClernand to continue moving south to the Disharoon plantation on the west bank of the river. Porter's battered fleet screened the passing of transports downriver past Grand Gulf.[12]

Grant must have been surprised, and perhaps shaken, by Bowen's strong stand, but he did not stop to worry about it; there were undefended landing spots a short distance downriver. He considered the port town of Rodney until information from slaves who lived along the river convinced him to choose a community, actually more like a ghost town, called Bruinsburg, which now consisted of nothing more than an occasional landing place for riverboats and provided an excellent location for Grant's purposes.

On the night of April 30, McClernand's troops boarded a hodge-podge of transports for the trip across to Mississippi. Officers tried to hurry this large amphibious operation, for they understood that Bowen might be redeploying to challenge the landing, and Bowen did indeed begin shifting troops to the countryside west of Port Gibson. Getting them there from Grand Gulf took a great deal of time, however, and Pemberton's slow realization of Grant's intentions meant that even when Bowen arrived, he would be heavily outnumbered. Despite the Grand Gulf repulse, Grant's campaign was proceeding according to plan. The diversionary tactics that had caused Pemberton to scatter his troops meant that Grant's army would outnumber whatever enemy force tried to block its march inland.[13]

The month of April had indeed been a good one for Grant, give or take a misgiving or two. His transfer of men south had gone well; his officers and men had overcome numerous glitches in the march downstream; and Porter's navy had performed wonderfully in moving transports below Vicksburg and Grand Gulf to make the army's crossing of the Mississippi possible. Diversions by Steele, Sherman, and, especially, Grierson had thrown an inexperienced Pemberton into a total state of confusion; further, Pemberton possessed not a smidgen of Grant's self-confidence. If Grant seemed indecisive at times, and he often had, he nevertheless constantly

sought opportunities to gain an advantage over opposing commanders. The various plans he had tried since January, hoping for
some sort of breakthrough, had been disappointing, but he never
stopped searching for the one that would work. Now, seizing the
moment that resulted from daring planning and an unsettled opponent, he felt sure that he was at last on the right course. There
had been times in his career when he might have pulled back after
events forced him to abandon his plan to use Grand Gulf as a base.
But following his decision to send McClernand south, his overall
concept of getting his army downriver had gone along unimpeded,
overcoming flooded roads and generally feeble Rebel resistance. It
seemed he could now smell victory, for surely his success so far
would draw more support from Washington, and with that support he was convinced that nothing would stop him and his army
until at last Vicksburg fell and gave the Union control of the
Mississippi.

Indeed, the outlook along the lower Mississippi seemed very
positive for the Union cause. Grant's trailblazing army moving
south along the Louisiana side of the river had established bases
that would be used as staging areas for supplies and posts for reinforcements to cordon that side. The presence of this Union line made
it difficult for Pemberton to get help from west of the Mississippi,
and the Confederate government added to his problems by refusing to insist that their reluctant generals in the trans-Mississippi
area cooperate with him. The faulty Confederate departmental
structure along the river assisted Grant in ways that he did not
then know about but came to appreciate.

Grant recalled his feelings as his troops moved onto Mississippi soil:

> When this was effected I felt a degree of relief scarcely ever
> equaled since. Vicksburg was not yet taken it is true, nor were its
> defenders demoralized by any of our previous moves. I was now
> in the enemy's country, with a vast river and the stronghold of
> Vicksburg between me and my base of supplies. But I was on dry
> ground on the same side of the river with the enemy. All the cam-
> paigns, labors, hardships and exposures from the month of De-
> cember previous to this time that had been made and endured,
> were for the accomplishment of this one object.[14]

The next immediate challenge would be gaining a solid foothold in Mississippi. While troops continued crossing the river, the
advance of McClernand's corps marched inland, with Eugene Carr's

division in the lead. They did not know what awaited them, but for a time the moonlit night seemed peaceable and the terrain much drier than the ground they had crossed in Louisiana. Soon, however, the road inland inclined upward, and Iowa troops leading the way found themselves among steep hills and dales. These men were experienced enough to know that such terrain made good defensive positions. Might these bluffs conceal the enemy? They and the unassuming, unpretentious, innovative, and determined general who had gotten them this far would find out before morning.[15]

NOTES

1. *OR*, ser. 1, vol. 24, pt. 3, p. 126; pt. 1, p. 22.
2. Ibid., pt. 3, p. 151; pt. 1, p. 46.
3. On the Duckport Canal see Bearss, *Vicksburg*, 2:43–51.
4. *OR*, ser. 1, vol. 24, pt. 1, p. 28; pt. 3, p. 92.
5. Bearss, *Vicksburg*, 2:269–89 passim.
6. *OR*, ser. 1, vol. 24, pt. 3, p. 152; pt. 1, p. 26; *Official Records of the Union and Confederate Navies in the War of the Rebellion*, 35 vols. (Washington, DC, 1894–1927), ser. 1, vol. 24, p. 520 (hereafter cited as *ORN* followed by series number, volume number, and page numbers).
7. *OR*, ser. 1, vol. 24, pt. 3, pp. 713–14; pt. 1, pp. 490–92.
8. Ibid., pt. 1, pp. 76–78; *ORN*, ser. 1, vol. 24, p. 555; Grant, *Memoirs*, 306–7; Bearss, *Vicksburg*, 2:57–58, 101.
9. See Bearss, *Vicksburg*, 2:107–26 (Steele's expedition), 253–68 (Sherman's diversion).
10. *OR*, ser. 1, vol. 24, pt. 1, p. 34. The standard account is D. Alexander Brown, *Grierson's Raid* (Dayton, OH, 1981).
11. *OR*, ser. 1, vol. 24, pt. 3, pp. 204–5, 211, 237–38; Bearss, *Vicksburg*, 2:271–74, 277, 285–89.
12. *ORN*, ser. 1, vol. 24, pp. 607–28 passim; Fred Grant, "General Ulysses S. Grant: His Son's Memories of Him in the Field," *National Tribune*, January 20, 1887.
13. *OR*, ser. 1, vol. 24, pt. 1, p. 48; Grant, *Memoirs*, 317–18; Bearss, *Vicksburg*, 2:318.
14. Grant, *Memoirs*, 321.
15. *OR*, ser. 1, vol. 24, pt. 1, pp. 143, 615, 628.

CHAPTER NINE

FIGHTING TO REACH VICKSBURG

THE COUNTRYSIDE THAT Federal troops encountered as they penetrated the hills west of Port Gibson inspired Grant to describe it as standing "on edge, as it were, the roads running along the ridges except when they occasionally pass from one ridge to another. Where there are no clearings the sides of the hills are covered with a very heavy growth of timber and with undergrowth, and the ravines are filled with vines and canebrakes, almost impenetrable." Grant understood that in battle on this sort of terrain, even if he outnumbered the Confederates, geography could help the enemy delay his push into interior Mississippi.[1]

His evaluation summed up the situation succinctly. John Bowen had some 8,000 men to confront 24,000 Union troops (McClernand's corps and a portion of McPherson's), yet he held them up throughout most of May 1. A few, but not nearly enough, troops arrived from Vicksburg to reinforce Bowen, but Grant's masterful strategy of diversion had deprived the Confederates of sufficient strength to make a significant stand, friendly terrain notwithstanding. The road Grant's army took toward Port Gibson divided near the Shaifer home, where fighting erupted shortly after midnight, April 30–May 1. The night fighting was spectacular and indecisive, but it gave Bowen more time to bring troops over from Grand Gulf and to deploy defensive lines on both roads.

The major portion of McClernand's corps, minus Peter Osterhaus's division, pushed the Confederates east along the main road, while Osterhaus, eventually reinforced by McPherson's troops, fought Bowen's right wing on the other road that forked to the northeast. Eventually, numbers told: by day's end, Bowen had no choice but to pull back; otherwise, he would have been flanked and perhaps have lost his whole force. Predictably, Grant in his memoirs gave most of the credit for the victory to Osterhaus's and McPherson's soldiers, paying almost no attention to McClernand's role. In fact, McClernand had fought well, using his overwhelming numbers to steamroll the Confederates in his front, forcing Bowen's

left wing to fall back to a creek bottom. After additional hard fighting, McClernand's raw power sent the Rebels retreating toward Port
Gibson. The Confederate right fared no better, but Bowen managed
to get most of his survivors there out of harm's way, across Bayou
Pierre, and the rearguard burned the bayou bridge behind them.[2]

Grant, as he had said he would, rode with McClernand, who
was also accompanied by Governor Richard Yates and Congressman Elihu Washburne of Illinois, the latter Grant's longtime bene-
factor. After the initial defeat of Rebel forces in his front around
Magnolia Church, an exuberant McClernand shouted victory, while
Grant gritted his teeth and then quietly remarked that the battle
was not yet over. True, the Rebels had fallen back, but there was no
indication that they had completely given up the field, as indeed
they had not. Then McClernand led his men forward to deliver the
knockout blow.[3]

Was Grant riding with McClernand because he did not trust
him, as some observers, drawing from Grant's hints, have concluded? Perhaps, but it is just as likely that Grant wanted to be
with Washburne, for he certainly understood by now the importance of keeping politicians, especially this one, happy. And even
though Grant's bitterness toward McClernand had been festering
for a long time, he had trusted him enough to take the lead and
soon had him in command of the important left wing as the army
marched northeast into interior Mississippi.

The long-held historical view that Grant thought McClernand
an incompetent buffoon who had to be tolerated solely because of
his political connections simply is not supported by the facts of the
campaign. True, McClernand's performance so far had not been
flawless; for example, he did not see to it that his men had sufficient rations before they moved inland from the river toward Port
Gibson. Yet despite such an oversight and his grating personality,
McClernand managed for the most part to do his job and do it well.
Grant believed strongly enough in the cause he fought for not to
let his personal feelings interfere with using his subordinates where
they best served his and the army's needs. Thus, he kept McClernand around as long as the outcome of the campaign was in doubt;
not until victory seemed assured did he find a way to get rid of
him. When that happened, he still had Sherman and McPherson,
and there were junior officers who showed much promise. But for
now, the operation needed continuity, and McClernand was a key
cog in the Federal machine.

Grant's army performed admirably, and they sensed they were rolling toward victory. The men—mostly midwesterners, as were their officers—took pride in their success, and they cheered their Illinois leaders, John Logan and McClernand, and McPherson, the Ohioan. They also waved their hats and yelled when slovenly Sam Grant came into view. He was one of them, a man who battled misfortunes as they had battled the frontier. These men were as hard as they were unpretentious, and they sensed the same qualities in their commander. They had come a long way together since northern Mississippi, and now good things were happening.

Once the Rebels fled Port Gibson, Grant, impatient with waiting for his engineers to put a new bridge across Bayou Pierre, ordered McPherson to send one of his brigades in search of another crossing. Finding one, these troops moved north by northeast as an advance, while McClernand's corps began crossing the bayou over the new bridge.

Grant gave little serious thought to sending help to Nathaniel Banks in the Port Hudson area. He was not about to give up transportation on the Mississippi to assist Banks. Grant needed every boat he had to get all his army across and to stockpile supplies at Grand Gulf. Anyway, in Grant's view, Banks seemed to be wandering about Louisiana accomplishing nothing rather than focusing on the job at hand: clearing the Mississippi. Grant so notified Halleck and turned his attention to his inland march. He would not get a response for several days, and by then Halleck would hardly be in a position to chastise him. Being a long way from Washington continued to be advantageous.[4]

Beyond his suspicion of Banks's ability, Grant understood the necessity of getting inland quickly. Trying to get in touch with Banks would cost time. Grant fully expected Pemberton to send more troops to stop him, and before that happened, he wanted to get his forces into Grand Gulf—abandoned by Bowen—so that with the help of Porter's sailors a supply depot could be established there. Despite his later claim that he cut himself loose from his supply base when he entered Mississippi, Grant soon had a large stockpile of goods at Grand Gulf, and wagon trains bearing food and ammunition followed the army inland. The line of depots along the Louisiana side of the river had been stocked with food and munitions, brought by river from the north, and all these supplies could now be sent on to Grand Gulf. Sherman, as his corps trailed the rest of the army, helped set up the supply line. The lesson of Holly Springs remained clear, and Grant did not intend to be totally cut off from his supplies again. He might be leaving his base, but he was fully determined to maintain an umbilical cord of wagons connecting it to his army.[5]

Once he was satisfied with work on the supply depot, Grant turned his attention once again to moving his army toward Vicksburg. As his troops marched northeast, brushing aside occasional Confederate resistance, he had in mind pushing north to Edwards Station, which lay along the Southern Railroad of Mississippi just east of where the rail line crossed the Big Black River. Grant envisioned straddling the railroad and pushing west toward Vicksburg, forcing Pemberton either to fight in the open, to abandon Vicksburg, or to withdraw into the city, where he would in effect be trapped.

To prevent the enemy from understanding what he intended, Grant turned to the tactic of diversions that had already worked so well and continued to play a role in the Federal army's march north. For example, the Big Black ran southwest from Edwards Station before emptying into the Mississippi above Grand Gulf. Several ferries operated along that river, and Grant had no doubt that Pemberton would have troops watching any such crossings potentially available to Union forces. So he sent a detachment in the direction of Warrenton, Vicksburg's southern flank, and patrols to reconnoiter the ferries. Again, such moves forced Pemberton to keep his forces spread out. While he kept the Confederate commander on edge, Grant ordered reinforcements to start from upriver for Grand Gulf. Sherman was already on the way from his demonstration up the Yazoo, but Grant wanted to concentrate as many troops as possible while the Confederates dispersed, guessing what the Yankees might do next.[6]

McClernand, marching his corps on the left as the main body of the army pushed north by northeast toward central Mississippi, was easily in the most dangerous position, for if Pemberton should get aggressive and send troops across the Big Black, they would attack McClernand's left flank. Grant therefore made sure that cavalry patrols stayed between McClernand's left and the Big Black to sound a warning. He did not want any surprise flank and rear assaults.

Grant need not have been overly concerned, for he faced a defensive-minded general who was receiving many intelligence reports that were either totally faulty or very misleading. Lacking precise information, Pemberton spent a lot of time trying to predict where the Federals would go. The enemy once more aided Grant when Jefferson Davis decided to keep troops at Port Hudson rather than abandoning that place to reinforce a desperate Pemberton. Of course, if the Confederates had deserted Port Hudson, Banks would have been free to reinforce Grant, but given Banks's reputation for making questionable campaign decisions, Grant would probably not have been entirely happy to see him.[7]

In any event, Grant pushed on, though slowing the pace to wait for Sherman, who, because of delays involving boat transportation, had been later than expected getting his troops across the Mississippi, having begun the effort on May 2. Finally, on May 7, Sherman had his corps in Mississippi and was preparing to move northeast to catch up. His troops would take the center of Grant's march, with McPherson on the right. At least Sherman's late arrival allowed his corps to help protect the wagon train supply line against occasional Rebel cavalry raids. Sherman worried perhaps even more than Grant about supplies, and he sent Grant a note warning that the depot at Grand Gulf was not as well organized as it ought to be. To remedy that situation would require more time than Grant wanted to allow, so he told Sherman that the army would have to be more aggressive in foraging. He could not and would not give Pemberton more time to receive reinforcements by waiting for Sherman to straighten out the problems at Grand Gulf.

If Pemberton and his officers had had any kind of foresight, they would have ordered supplies taken away or destroyed along Grant's line of advance; the absence of food along the way would certainly have slowed the Union march as troops waited for wagons coming up from Grand Gulf. Again, Grant was aided by the inexperience and ineptness of his opponent.[8] Depending on enemy territory for food, however, could create morale problems among Grant's troops. Union forces in the advance had top choice of local supplies, leaving slim pickings indeed for those coming up later. Thus, many of Grant's men had to exist on short rations, since the heavy, slow wagon trains from Grand Gulf could not keep up with the army, and rainy weather that turned the poor Mississippi roads into quagmires further held up their progress.

As foraging increased, soldiers sometimes not only sought out food but also wrecked homes, especially if they found them empty. Grant, who had once worried about such behavior, did not seem

James B. McPherson. From the National Archives

overly concerned. Yet the army appeared to be losing some of its discipline, for the march encountered little resistance and ample opportunities to raid private structures and property. On May 12, with Sherman at last on hand, Grant issued marching instructions for his three corps, expecting that firmer orders would prevent destructive behavior by the men. Until this time, the army had advanced more like a scouting detachment than an invading force, because Grant was feeling his way, reaching sure he had a proper handle on the situation before making hard decisions about his route and targets. Now he wanted more precise marches.[9]

On the left, McClernand proceeded toward Edwards Station to the north before turning west along Telegraph Road; one division covered the corps's left flank. Sherman marched on McClernand's right toward a place called Dillon's Plantation, between the town of Raymond and Edwards Station, and McPherson headed toward Raymond, which lay a few miles southwest of the capital city of Jackson. Grant, apparently deciding he no longer had to look over McClernand's shoulder and no doubt eager for more compatible company, rode with his friend Sherman and on the evening of the twelfth set up his headquarters in the Dillon home. Despite occasional skirmishing with some of John Bowen's troops, now deployed southeast of Edwards, McClernand's divisions managed to capture key fords and bridges in order to secure a direct route to the railroad.[10]

On the Union right, McPherson advanced leisurely toward Raymond, unaware that May 12 would be considerably more adventurous for his corps than for the other two. At the same time, John Pemberton learned that John Gregg and his brigade, reinforcements from Port Hudson—and the only ones he could expect, given Jefferson Davis's decision to hang on to that river bastion—had arrived in Jackson. Pemberton ordered Gregg to Raymond to watch for Grant's advance but otherwise had problems trying to coordinate his deployments to meet Grant's perceived routes, which, he assumed, correctly at the time, would be toward the railroad. Yet unknown to Pemberton, Grant's thinking remained flexible, a quality that would serve him well during the next few days.[11]

Gregg arrived in Raymond with instructions to hit the Union right flank and rear if the opportunity arose but not to bring on a general engagement if heavily outnumbered. His accidental disobedience of those orders caused the campaign to take a new turn, one neither Grant nor Pemberton expected. Gregg received reports from the scant cavalry available to him (vague orders from Pemberton had caused confusion about where his cavalry was supposed to be, relative to the Raymond area) that Union troops had been spotted coming up the Utica road, which ran southwest from Raymond toward Port Gibson.

When Gregg heard this news during the early hours of the twelfth, he decided from the nature of the erroneous cavalry intelligence that these troops must be only a patrol, perhaps a detachment screening the Union right or just a feint to confuse the Confederates. Either way, he thought, his brigade should be able to handle the situation, and he made a fateful decision to attack. Gregg deployed his troops south of Raymond and north of Fourteenmile Creek. Only after the battle was well under way, with his men more than holding their own, did he realize he had chosen to send them against vastly superior numbers.[12]

McPherson, rather than bludgeoning the Confederates, as he could have done, sent in his brigades piecemeal, but his numbers finally convinced Gregg that this was a much larger force than he had been led to believe. After several hours of hard, confused fighting on a dusty battlefield, Gregg had to pull back and retreat to Jackson. His ill-fated decision had cost the Rebels more men, for now he would be cut off from Pemberton's main force in the Edwards Station area.

James McPherson won the fight, though he had not fought particularly well, but more important, the battle at Raymond caused Grant to reassess his strategy. When he received word of the conflict the evening of the twelfth at his Dillon home headquarters, he suddenly realized that striking the railroad and turning west without knowing how many enemy troops were in the Jackson area could be very risky. While Pemberton was being dealt with at Edwards Station, troops from Jackson could march west and attack the Union rear. Grant also had received news that the veteran Confederate general Joseph E. Johnston was now commanding troops in Jackson. Grant did not hesitate; he gave no thought to retreating—he had come too far and had been through too much to turn back now—the army would take care of Jackson and Johnston first and then attend to Pemberton. Grant had seen enough of Pemberton's inaction to believe that he could safely turn his back on the Rebels at Edwards Station. Just in case, however, McClernand's corps would countermarch from its proximity to Edwards back to Raymond to watch the Raymond-Edwards corridor for any Rebel aggression, while Sherman and McPherson marched to attack Jackson.[13]

McPherson went north to Clinton, several miles west of Jackson on the railroad, where he turned east; Sherman approached the city from the south. Rainy weather slowed the Union pincer movement, but ultimately their attacks prevailed, in large part because Johnston had no intention of fighting. Had he made a strong stand, significant reinforcements from the east might well have had time to reach Jackson. Instead, by leaving only a skeleton force to delay Sherman and McPherson while he evacuated Jackson and moved north toward Canton, Johnston cost the Confederacy more than a state capital.[14]

Grant continued riding with Sherman and was on hand when Sherman sent a detachment off to his right to flank the city's Confederate works. Union soldiers found little more than a token Rebel contingent, which surrendered immediately. While triumphant Yankees spilled into the streets of Jackson, Grant, Sherman, and McPherson met and celebrated at the Bowman House, a hotel close to the capitol building. While there, Grant received a copy of a Johnston-to-Pemberton message delivered by a Union spy—possibly an Illinois soldier named Charles Bell, acting as a Confederate courier— instructing Pemberton to come to Clinton and merge forces.[15]

Grant decided that with Johnston having fled, Pemberton should be attacked before the two Rebel wings were able to concentrate; he could not be sure that Johnston would not swing west, once out of Jackson, in an effort to find Pemberton. It would not be clear until a few days later just how brilliant Grant's decision to attack the capital had been, thanks to Johnston's actions. By taking himself out of the campaign, and having eliminated the opportunity for reinforcements to make a timely arrival by abandoning the railroad at Jackson, Johnston made Grant's task much easier.

As things turned out, Grant had little to worry about, but at the time he had no way of knowing that Johnston would go on to Canton, or that Pemberton was going to march southeast from Edwards Station in search of Grant's supply wagons, or that it would thus be impossible for Pemberton and Johnston to get together at any time soon, especially with Grant's army positioned between them. Acting on what he did know, Grant sent McPherson hurrying west to Bolton, another town on the railroad just east of Edwards, while Sherman stayed behind to destroy anything that the Confederates might find useful in Jackson.[16]

John Pemberton had vacillated after receiving Johnston's message about coming to Clinton. He knew that Union troops (McClernand's corps) were still somewhere toward Raymond, so if his forces moved east from Edwards Station, they risked being hit in the right flank and defeated, thus opening the way to Vicksburg. Pemberton adhered to the defense of Vicksburg to the last, as instructed by President Davis, whereas Johnston had decided upon his arrival in Jackson that the safety of Confederate troops mattered more than the city on the river. Pemberton and his generals held a council of war, and he finally agreed with a suggestion that he go to Raymond to find and destroy Grant's supply wagons. The march toward Raymond turned into a logistical fiasco, and by the night of May 15, his army was strung out from near an eminence called Champion Hill on its left to the Raymond road on the right. Next morning, Pemberton received a second message from Johnston, which detailed the evacuation of Jackson and again ordered Pemberton to come on to Clinton. Johnston, however, made no effort to meet Pemberton there, a fact Pemberton was not aware of when he ordered his army to reverse its course to the north and east. With Jackson in enemy hands, Pemberton had obviously decided that he should follow Johnston's instructions this time, just to protect himself in case anything went wrong. While Pemberton's Confederates were preparing to countermarch, two of Grant's three corps, McPherson's and McClernand's, attacked.[17]

Grant had earlier ridden to Clinton and issued orders for the convergence of the two corps on Pemberton's position. McClernand spread his men on the Raymond road, the Middle road (between the Jackson road to the north and the Raymond road), and the Jackson road to Edwards Station (he already had his troops on the move before receiving written instructions). McPherson's corps moved east on the Jackson road behind Hovey's division of McClernand's corps. Grant also sent word to Sherman to wrap things up in Jackson and bring his corps east as soon as possible.

These quick movements caught Pemberton totally off balance. Despite the large number of campfires visible to the east the night of May 15, he seemed unable to grasp that enemy troops blocked the Raymond road and were in position to come after him where he was. When skirmishing broke out early on May 16 on the Raymond road, Pemberton still did not understand that he had to make a stand. Then, when a courier arrived with Johnston's message about evacuating Jackson and reiterating his instruction to join forces, Pemberton proceeded to order the clumsy maneuver of reversing his army to go to Clinton. Meanwhile, William Loring, commanding a division on Pemberton's right, asked and received permission to form a line of battle on the Raymond road. Then John

BATTLE OF CHAMPION HILL
May 16, 1863

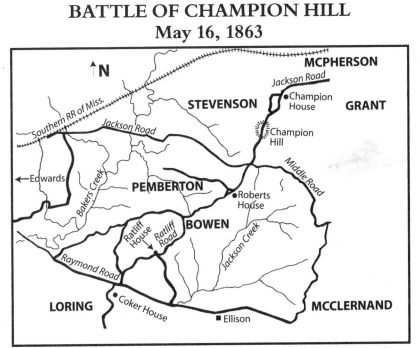

Adapted from Michael B. Ballard, *Pemberton: A Biography* (Jackson: University Press of Mississippi, 1991), 161.

Bowen in the center deployed along the Middle road, and finally Carter Stevenson on the left had to stop trying to countermarch and face Hovey's advance on the Jackson road. Pemberton's wagon train in the rear was moved out of harm's way north of the railroad but too far from the army to keep it resupplied with ammunition.[18]

Grant's broad approach forced Pemberton to accept the obvious truth that he could not withdraw without exposing the entire long line of his army to a Federal flank attack; he had to give battle or be routed. As the fighting developed, the Union forces made moderate progress on the Raymond and Middle roads, for they had been told to advance with caution earlier in the day; on the Federal right, Hovey, supported by McPherson's entire corps, gave Stevenson's division a severe whipping.

As McPherson hurried the troops forward, Grant, riding along with the XVII Corps, encouraged McPherson's men to keep up the pressure. But because the ongoing fighting and the hilly country-side made communication slow, Grant did not issue strong attack orders to commanders in his center and on his left. McClernand was told to press hard if the opportunity arose. In battle conditions he had an implied right to act aggressively on his own, but if he did so and blundered, he had to know how hard Grant would come down on him. Thus, the Union right, where Grant saw what was happening and issued orders accordingly, made greater progress. Grant might have coordinated the battle better, getting more equal pressure across the front, if he had positioned himself on the Middle road and established a courier system to the two flanks. His messengers would have had less ground to cover riding to the right and left from a central point, and coordination of the fighting might have been more effective.

Another interesting point is Grant's preference to ride first with Sherman and then McPherson after the army began moving inland from Port Gibson. Obviously he preferred their company, despite his earlier indication that he would stay with McClernand to keep an eye on him, but if he was concerned about McClernand's ability, he should have at least ridden over to check on him. McClernand, though Grant implied otherwise in his memoirs, had performed well at Port Gibson, had shielded the army's march northeast and had guarded its rear while the other two corps attacked Jackson. Though Grant could not bring himself to say anything good about him, his actions had shown more respect for McClernand's ability than he ever admitted.

The Union right enjoyed great success in the spirited attack on Pemberton's left; Grant at one point sent division commander John Logan a note of congratulations for making history by sending the enemy fleeing. The decimation of Stevenson's division forced Pemberton to order help from his center and his right, despite the dangers posed by Union troops in those sectors. Loring stubbornly refused to move, arguing that to do so would open the Raymond road to the enemy and risk the flanking of the battle line. Bowen in the center also hesitated, but once he realized the extent of the disaster on the left, which threatened his own left flank, he pulled out most of his division and led a charge against the Union center.

Bowen's charge proved to be the most spectacular of the battle and one of the most impressive of the war. His Missourians and Arkansans routed Union troops and penetrated all the way to the crest of Champion Hill and beyond. Pemberton had no reserves to send in support, however, whereas Grant helped rush reinforcements forward to stop the Rebels and mend the breach of the Union center. Bowen's attack was the Confederate high-water mark at

Champion Hill. As he pulled back, pressure increased along the Union center and left, and soon Pemberton, realizing the day was lost, ordered a retreat, but the collapse of the Confederate left limited his options for pulling back. Loring acted as rearguard for the army, most of which had to escape along the Raymond road. Loring was eventually cut off and forced to take a roundabout route to Jackson and Canton in order to link up with Johnston's army.[19]

Grant wanted the Confederates pursued; he no doubt believed his victory so decisive that he perhaps could end the campaign by destroying Pemberton's army as a cohesive unit. Since his left had not experienced heavy fighting, Grant ordered Eugene Carr's division of McClernand's corps to lead the pursuit. Meanwhile, one of McPherson's divisions did some chasing of its own but was slowed by Confederate rearguard action. McClernand urged his men on as he, too, sensed the possibility of a general surrender of Pemberton's forces, but the lateness of the day and strong Rebel resistance prevented the complete Federal victory that seemed so close at hand. By nightfall, however, Grant's advance had occupied Edwards Station, and the surviving Confederates had fallen back to their works east of the Big Black. There Pemberton ordered a halt while he waited for Loring to show up; unfortunately for the Confederates, he had not been informed that Loring was marching his division to Jackson. Loring got away, leaving Bowen's tired division to face Grant's oncoming troops the next day, May 17, for no good reason. Stevenson's survivors had already crossed the Big Black, and soon his and Bowen's units streamed toward Vicksburg, where two fresh divisions awaited them.[20]

Grant continued his aggressive tactics at the Big Black. He sent Sherman across the river at Bridgeport, north of the railroad, to get on the flank and rear of Pemberton's army. One of Sherman's brigades guarded Grant's supply wagons; while part of McPherson's corps mopped up the battlefield at Champion Hill, the rest arrived and camped near Edwards Station on the seventeenth, too late to fight at the Big Black. That left McClernand's corps to assault the Confederates, and his troops did a good job of it, effectively scattering Bowen's demoralized force toward and into the river. Across the river, two Rebel brigades provided much-needed cover fire, which allowed many of Bowen's men to escape.

While the one-sided battle raged, a satisfied Grant watched and then looked with amusement at a dispatch handed him from Halleck, dated May 11. Halleck wanted Grant to pull back to Grand

Gulf and cooperate with Banks. Commenting wryly that he did not think he could obey such instructions just now, Grant folded the note and put it in a coat pocket. Both he and Banks soon had enough to occupy their attention without worrying about supporting each other.[21]

Pemberton might have escaped to the north, saving his army, but with Davis's admonition about the necessity of holding Vicksburg firmly ground into his psyche, he chose instead to withdraw into the city's defenses. Grant later criticized that choice and argued that he would have let Pemberton go in peace in order to get Vicksburg. By sending Sherman to Bridgeport, and eventually McPherson to Amsterdam, located on the river south of Bridgeport and north of the Big Black railroad crossing, Grant gave the impression that he expected Pemberton to turn north to get away. If that happened, two of Grant's three corps would be in a position to contest such a march. If Pemberton had made that move, would he have ordered the two divisions in Vicksburg to evacuate the city and march to a junction with Johnston? Such a question never came up, because Pemberton never considered it, but the possibility is intriguing.

Grant understood the political and psychological necessity of taking Vicksburg, but whether he would have let Pemberton take four divisions, move uncontested to the east, and concentrate with Johnston is debatable, given his troop dispositions at Big Black. It does not seem that capturing Vicksburg while allowing a significant Confederate force to remain loose in central Mississippi would have been a realistic scenario, for Vicksburg could not be secure until Pemberton and Johnston were neutralized, and Grant would have been the one assigned to that job. Grant later speculated that if he had captured Pemberton's army in Vicksburg quickly, he would have turned a portion of the Union army east to pursue Johnston.

Also with the benefit of hindsight, and as a result of his negative feelings toward McClernand, which never softened, Grant criticized his subordinate after the war for not fighting more aggressively at Champion Hill. Yet McClernand had only followed Grant's orders, which clearly urged caution for most of the day. Much of the problem could be traced to Grant's view of the fighting, limited by his location on the army's right. Communications difficulties were reminiscent of the Iuka campaign, when he was too far from the action to make realistic assessments. Later, with time to reflect, Grant no doubt realized that a hard push all along his battlefront at Champion Hill could well have destroyed Pemberton's army, but that was "what if" thinking, and the lost opportunity could not be fairly laid at McClernand's feet. McClernand had followed Grant's orders and moved aggressively on the Raymond road when told to do so, but he had been told much too late.[22]

How much, if any, of this flowed through Grant's mind at the time, as his army pushed on past the Big Black toward Vicksburg, is not known; his mood seemed mostly upbeat. Even though the Confederates burned both the railroad bridge and the boat that served as a bridge, thereby delaying McClernand's crossing of the Big Black, all three corps—McClernand's on the left, McPherson's in the center, and Sherman's on the right—were soon marching toward Vicksburg. The army maintained that basic alignment during coming operations on the city's perimeter. So far, Pemberton had eluded the killing blow, but Grant had every reason to be optimistic. With the exception of Bowen's performance, both at Port Gibson and at Champion Hill, he had seen little about this Southern army that was impressive. Vicksburg should very shortly be in Union hands.

Grant discussed with Sherman his basic idea for approaching Vicksburg: Sherman's corps would form the right and confront the Rebel lines that arched roughly northwest toward the Mississippi. The Graveyard road would be his marching route, though he would guard the Jackson road until McPherson arrived and deployed in the center along a line that extended south from Sherman's left toward the railroad. McClernand would be positioned south of the railroad, with his troops extending the battle line farther south. Obviously, Grant had learned much about the Vicksburg area and Pemberton's defenses, both from white scouts who acted as spies and from slaves eager to help the Union army.

Sherman listened intently to these plans and then congratulated Grant. He admitted that he had never thought the idea of crossing below Vicksburg would work, but obviously he had been wrong. Vicksburg was yet to be taken, but the army had made it to a point that had seemed impossible not so long ago. One can only wonder if the thought crossed Grant's mind that the one man who had strongly supported the plan, John McClernand, had played a key role in its success. Probably not, for McClernand's persona made

it difficult to think good thoughts about him, especially for someone like Grant who had been victimized by McClernand's machinations.[23]

Certainly, Sherman was right about one thing; the campaign
had been a success, regardless of what happened next. Grant,
Sherman, McClernand, and McPherson soon learned, however, that
a crippled enemy did not necessarily mean a defeated enemy. Before Vicksburg fell, much fighting and dying remained.

NOTES

1. Grant, *Memoirs*, 322–23.
2. On the battle near Port Gibson see Bearss, *Vicksburg*, 2:317–20, 345–
401.
3. *OR*, ser. 1, vol. 24, pt. 1, pp. 145, 603; Bearss, *Vicksburg*, 2:385–86.
4. *OR*, ser. 1, vol. 24, pt. 3, p. 262; pt. 1, pp. 635, 653, 706; Bearss,
Vicksburg, 2:432–35; Simpson, *Grant*, 183; James Pickett Jones, *Blackjack:
John A. Logan and Southern Illinois in the Civil War Era* (Carbondale, IL,
1995), 158, 166.
5. *OR*, ser. 1, vol. 24, pt. 1, pp. 33, 49; Bearss, *Vicksburg*, 2:437; Bernard
Schermerhorn to Josie, May 5, 1863, Schermerhorn Papers, Indiana Historical Society, Indianapolis; Grant, *Memoirs*, 328; Marszalek, *Sherman*, 221.
6. *OR*, ser. 1, vol. 24, pt. 3, pp. 268–69; pt. 2, pp. 12, 133; pt. 1, p. 50.
7. Bearss, *Vicksburg*, 2:452; Michael B. Ballard, *Pemberton: A Biography*
(Jackson, MS, 1991), 143.
8. *OR*, ser. 1, vol. 24, pt. 2, p. 254; pt. 3, pp. 277–78, 285–86.
9. Ibid., pt. 3, pp. 296–97, 299; pt. 1, pp. 50, 146–47; Samuel I. Sneier to
Sir, June 21, 1863, Sneier Papers, Indiana Historical Society.
10. *OR*, ser. 1, vol. 24, pt. 3, pp. 296–97, 299; pt. 1, pp. 47, 50.
11. Ballard, *Pemberton*, 149–50.
12. Ibid., 150; *OR*, ser. 1, vol. 24, pt. 3, pp. 855–66 passim.
13. Bearss, *Vicksburg*, 2:512–13; on the battle of Raymond see 483–514.
14. *OR*, ser. 1, vol. 24, pt. 1, pp. 50–51; Grant, *Memoirs*, 332; on the
battle of Jackson see Bearss, *Vicksburg*, 2:519–55.
15. Grant, *Memoirs*, 337–38; Feis, *Grant's Secret Service*, 162.
16. *OR*, ser. 1, vol. 24, pt. 1, pp. 51, 639, 754.
17. Ballard, *Pemberton*, 154–59.
18. Ibid., 160–62; *OR*, ser. 1, vol. 24, pt. 1, pp. 51–52, 730.
19. Ulysses S. Grant, "The Vicksburg Campaign," in *Battles and Leaders of the Civil War*, 4 vols., ed. Robert Underwood Johnson and Clarence
Clough Buell (New York, 1956), 3:511. On Champion Hill see Bearss,
Vicksburg, 2:559–641.
20. Ballard, *Pemberton*, 164–65; *OR*, ser. 1, vol. 24, pt. 1, pp. 53, 150–51;
Grant, *Memoirs*, 349–50.
21. Ballard, *Pemberton*, 165–66; Grant, *Memoirs*, 350. On the battle at
Big Black see Bearss, *Vicksburg*, 2:653–85.
22. Grant, *Memoirs*, 347, 349.
23. Ibid., 354–55, 364; Sherman, *Memoirs*, 250.

Chapter Ten

Assault, Siege, and Surrender

AS BOTH SIDES readied for the coming assault, Sherman's corps made contact with David Porter's vessels on the Yazoo, thereby opening a supply line that delighted Grant's soldiers, who had subsisted largely on hardtack longer than they cared to think about. Admiral Porter had tired of duty around the Red River and Port Hudson and had brought part of his fleet back up to Vicksburg, now that the current had slowed, to get in on the action and to rejoin his friends Sherman and Grant.

As he pondered the final phase of the campaign, Grant considered the mood of his men. They had formed a bond of trust with him, and they had cheered him on the battlefields. If they had not placed him on some high pedestal, they often stood in respect when he passed by. He had brought them a long way, and they believed in him and fully anticipated taking Vicksburg soon. He may have had some doubts, and many of his men may themselves have wondered whether the impressive-looking works they saw across the hills and ravines could be easily conquered. Yet most seemed to be in a mood to make the attempt, and Grant understood that he had to give them the opportunity to overwhelm Pemberton's army and end this long drive. He thought Confederate morale was such that resistance would be minimal and brief; moreover, he doubted that his men would embrace the rigors of a siege, if such became necessary, unless they had tested the Rebels first. So Grant let them try. On May 19 he issued attack orders.[1]

He soon learned that his confidence and pride in his army had overruled sound reasoning. Only Sherman's corps was close enough to enemy lines to have a good chance of carrying the Confederate works. McPherson's troops were still 1,000 yards or so from the Rebels in their front, and McClernand's men had to negotiate extremely rugged terrain before they could close on the defensive works south of the railroad. Added to all that, Sherman faced tough fighters, especially Bowen's Missourians, in the area of Stockade Redan, Pemberton's strong defenses on the Graveyard road.

Bowen's men still had their pride, not to mention sturdy defensive works, and they wanted to make amends for the Big Black embarrassment. Without the backing of the other two corps, Sherman's soldiers faced a tough challenge.

Grant's eagerness for the attack and a quick conclusion to the campaign yielded him practically nothing but casualties. Charges against Stockade Redan proved suicidal, and, after absorbing heavy losses, Sherman accepted failure. The attacks were poorly planned and coordinated. Ladders necessary for ascending enemy works were not available, and all in all, many Union soldiers paid the ultimate price for the exuberance of officers and men who thought the Rebels would easily give up. McPherson's corps did little to help, with only one brigade seeing significant action on the nineteenth. An Illinois regiment from that brigade advanced to within 100 yards of the main Confederate line before hot enemy fire forced the men to halt and dig in. Other units closed gaps between the lines, but the Confederates held firm. McClernand's entire corps, encountering one geographic obstacle after another, finally stopped to dig in, still some 400 yards from the Confederate works.

Though Grant admitted defeat, his army had at least pushed forward into better positions to continue pressing Pemberton's defenses. For the day, Union losses totaled 157 killed, 777 wounded, and 8 missing; enemy losses, though uncertain, apparently totaled some 200. The one-sided struggle gave Grant a firm indication that these Confederates could and would still fight. Despite the pounding they had taken at Champion Hill and Big Black, they occupied solid entrenchments, and their fighting spirit had survived. The Federals would have to earn the capture of Vicksburg.[2]

At his headquarters, located near Sherman's line, Grant mulled over the situation and decided on a second attack, but this time his thinking went deeper than a quick victory. He understood that a siege would force him to ask for reinforcements from troops needed for the Union cause in Tennessee and even Virginia, not to mention by Banks to the south. Too, the more quickly he ended the campaign, the sooner he could pursue Johnston, who was still lurking somewhere in his rear to the east. Grant's soldiers remained optimistic and deserved another, more effective chance to break Confederate resistance and force Pemberton to surrender his army.[3]

Before launching a second assault, Grant gave his army time to rest, concentrate, and consolidate progress made on the nineteenth.

Supplies continued flowing to the men from the Yazoo base. Artillery emplacements were carefully selected and fortified. Men who had been left behind to mop up the battlefields east of the Big Black began arriving; details dug approach works, and big guns began hammering key points in the Rebel lines. In the midst of all this, both McClernand's and McPherson's corps tried to inch closer to the defensive works so that when the next attack came, they would not have nearly as much ground to cover.

Grant sent one brigade beyond McClernand's positions to watch the Warrenton road, which led south out of town. He did not believe Pemberton would try to escape via that route, for such a path would place him at an even greater distance from Johnston. Also, Union forces at Grand Gulf, guarding the depot there, could come up and block Rebel passage. Grant therefore intended his deployment to keep Pemberton's forces spread along the Union front. And if the defenders did not cover the southern approaches strongly enough, the Federal brigade could move into town and get into Pemberton's rear. Grant doubted that Pemberton would order any kind of sortie to flank McClernand, and the mere possibility that McClernand could shift troops to his left toward the southwest should make Pemberton reluctant to pull men from that area to help out at other points along the perimeter. Pemberton had to keep his far right in mind or suffer the consequences. Grant's main targets of the next general assault, however, would be the daunting enemy works fronting his three corps; if the assault failed, he could take a second look at tactical possibilities on the city's southern flank.[4]

In the midst of all this activity, Grant and McClernand had another confrontation. Grant had ordered one of McClernand's divisions, Alvin P. Hovey's, to remain at the Big Black to guard crossings should any of Johnston's force show up. McClernand had not been informed, and so, quite naturally wanting Hovey with the rest of the corps before the next assault was launched, he ordered Hovey to march to Vicksburg. Grant was furious at the thought that the Big Black was not being covered. Actually, Hovey had left behind two companies, but Grant wanted at least a brigade there, so McClernand had to settle for half a division rather than a whole one. Had Grant sent his initial order to Hovey through McClernand, as protocol dictated, no such misunderstanding would have developed, and it is doubtful Grant would have bypassed Sherman or McPherson in such a manner. From this point on, the Grant-McClernand command relationship deteriorated at an accelerated pace.[5]

Grant issued orders for a general assault to take place on May 22. McClernand protested, arguing that massed attacks at key positions would be more effective, but Grant understood, if McClernand did not, that the terrain made such a tactic not only difficult but in most cases also impossible. Concentrating men in columns would leave attacking forces vulnerable to flanking fire from Confederates spread out along the entrenchments connecting their defensive works, and in any case, the rugged terrain made it unlikely that large numbers of troops could mass anywhere and make a coordinated attack. It would be better to spread out the assault, thus forcing the outnumbered Rebels to deploy over long distances. At some places, as in Sherman's front, the nature of the ground did encourage concentrated assaults because roads that approached Rebel works were the best avenues of attack. Yet Yankees bunched closely together would give the Confederates much easier targets. Geography was definitely a Pemberton ally.

As Union forces advanced on May 22, the Confederate lines held once more. Sherman's corps again found the going rough, and many of his men, especially early in the day, spent more time trying to maneuver into better positions than actually shooting at the enemy. Sherman's charges down the Graveyard road became a killing ground for Rebel infantry protected by the well-built Stockade Redan. McPherson's forces accomplished little more than pushing more closely to the works in their front; they did not penetrate far enough to come close to breaching enemy lines.

McClernand had more success. His troops went up against Stevenson's division, which had been put on the Confederate right to recuperate. Pemberton did not think they would see much action there, since he anticipated Grant attacking his center and left. Stevenson's troops gave a good account of themselves, but they were spread thin, and much shuffling had to be done to hold off Federal brigades. The Confederates had three identifiable works that caught McClernand's attention. From the Union right to left, they were the Second Texas Lunette, the Railroad Redoubt, and Square Fort.

As action heated up on his front, McClernand sent word to Grant that he needed McPherson's help on his right. McPherson's corps was more lightly engaged, relatively speaking, and McClernand thought a brigade or so from the XVII Corps would help carry

the day at the Second Texas Lunette. Grant refused the request—
which he likely would not have done had it come from one of his
other corps commanders—telling McClernand to draw from his
own reserve rather than asking for aid elsewhere. Actually, all of
McClernand's corps were already heavily engaged with the exception of one brigade, so he continued to badger Grant, and this time
he padded the truth: he said that his men had partial possession of
two forts, that U.S. flags were floating over both, and that a hard
charge would fracture Pemberton's line. Actually, his soldiers had
achieved such success only at the Railroad Redoubt, and even there
the occupation had been brief. His implication that the planting of
flags meant capture of real estate was patently untrue. Grant suspected that this all too typical bombast might be hollow, and he
again urged McClernand to make do rather than ordering
McPherson to provide relief. He told McClernand to send instead
for the brigade currently on the far left at the Warrenton front—
though he had to know that those troops could not possibly arrive
in time to do McClernand any good in this day's fight.[6]

Meanwhile, Grant shared the McClernand situation with
Sherman, and Sherman said he would renew his attack in order to
pen the Confederates along his front and keep them from shifting
to the Union left. Then, as Grant told McPherson to press forward,
there came another note from McClernand advising that his troops
had occupied Rebel trenches at several points, his forces were all
engaged (the one idle brigade still had not entered the fight), and
he desperately needed men. Unconvinced but tired of McClernand's
continuing requests, Grant told McPherson to send a division.

Sherman's new assault failed to produce positive results, as did
McPherson's efforts to make progress. The saber rattling no doubt
kept Rebel defenders in place, but if Pemberton had been forced,
he could have shifted troops to his right without endangering his
center and left. McPherson's division on loan to McClernand departed south around midafternoon, minus one brigade left to keep
the battle line stable. The dust kicked up by the marching men
alerted the Confederates, and Pemberton sent in reserves to his
right. McClernand divided up the reinforcements and ordered them
into battle, but their arrival caused some confusion among his commanders, and desperate combat by additional Confederates rushing to the scene saved the day for Pemberton.[7]

At the end of the twenty-second, McClernand had accomplished
more than Sherman and McPherson, but he had not made the

progress he claimed, as Grant quickly noted. The whole episode indicated how the mistrust that had long existed between the two men affected the effort to break Pemberton's lines at Vicksburg. If the Rebels could not be overwhelmed, as Grant had hoped, he still had his army in position to besiege the city and no longer needed McClernand's field expertise. It seemed only a matter of time until the festering relationship between the two came to a conclusion.

Grant's losses on May 22 underscored the problem of attacking well-entrenched defenders who were obviously not ready to call it quits. Union casualties included 502 killed, 2,550 wounded, and 147 missing; total Confederate losses numbered only around 500. Terrain and strong Confederate resistance had made Sherman's and McPherson's actions so ineffective that Pemberton had in fact needed only about half his force to repulse Grant's army. Porter's navy had lobbed shells into the Rebel rear but with little effect because, due to the high banks and bluffs, they were lobbed on a high arc, which gave the Confederates time to see the shells coming and get out of the way. The Confederates had had anxious moments only on their right, where reinforcements were needed to thwart McClernand. Grant blamed McClernand for adding to casualty lists, reasoning that by implying more success than he had indeed enjoyed, McClernand had led Sherman and McPherson to make renewed attacks that caused more men to be shot down for no good reason. In a strict sense, this analysis was accurate, but it was also true that McClernand's corps had clearly been more effective on May 22 than the other two.[8] Fuming and frustrated, Grant delayed arranging a truce so that the Union dead could be buried before they lay too long in the hot Mississippi sun. Not until Pemberton sent a message through the lines on May 25 suggesting a truce for interments, after he heard complaints about the stench, did Grant agree. For two and one-half hours, burial details went about their grisly work.[9]

Accepting reality, Grant brushed aside his disappointment and moved on to plans for a siege. He needed more troops, men who could come down the river and land safely on the Yazoo. He must have more guns; Porter's heavy weapons on his gunboats would do in the short term, and others could be sent downriver. He required engineers; having only four with his army, he ordered all his officers who had attended West Point—where they had been exposed to military engineering—to assist in implementing siege operations and show how much they had learned. Also, he looked to the north-northeast of Vicksburg for any movement by Johnston in the Mechanicsburg Corridor, that stretch of land between the Yazoo and the Big Black, which Johnston would likely choose if he came to Pemberton's rescue. Grant intended to be ready for him.[10]

While the armies settled in for a waiting game, the kind of warfare that the Federals could afford and the Confederates could not, Grant finally had the opportunity to rid himself of one irritation, McClernand, who handed Grant the means when he issued congratulatory orders to his corps. These were innocent enough; his men had fought an exemplary campaign, but trouble erupted when he added comments implying that Grant and the other corps commanders had not aided his attack on May 22. Unfortunately for McClernand, the document appeared in a Memphis newspaper and was brought to Sherman's attention by one of his officers. The publication of such military communications had been prohibited in 1862, and the penalty for violation was dismissal from the service. Sherman and McPherson complained about the incident to Grant, who demanded an explanation. McClernand admitted that the newspaper version was accurate and regretted that Grant had not been sent a copy, a lapse for which he blamed his adjutant. Grant was not impressed; using the authority to dismiss troublemakers given him by Secretary of War Stanton, on June 18 he relieved McClernand of his command and ordered E. O. C. Ord to take his place. McClernand complained loudly to Stanton, Lincoln, and any other political contact he could think of, but to no avail. If Grant had any lingering doubts about his standing in Washington, the sacking of McClernand without any interference confirmed the faith of the president and the War Department in him, or at least their lack of faith in McClernand. Whatever the case, they showed no hesitation in supporting Grant's decision.[11]

Union engineers and work details, meanwhile, were establishing entrenchments and planning approaches to enemy lines in a long semicircle from north of Vicksburg around to the south. Porter's navy controlled the riverfront and unnerved civilians and Pemberton's army with periodic shelling. Grant realized that by tightening the noose, he could block most attempts by Johnston or anyone else to get food or munitions to Pemberton's army. Once all seemed ready, his growing army started pushing closer to enemy lines, giving the Rebels little time to rest and forcing them to con-

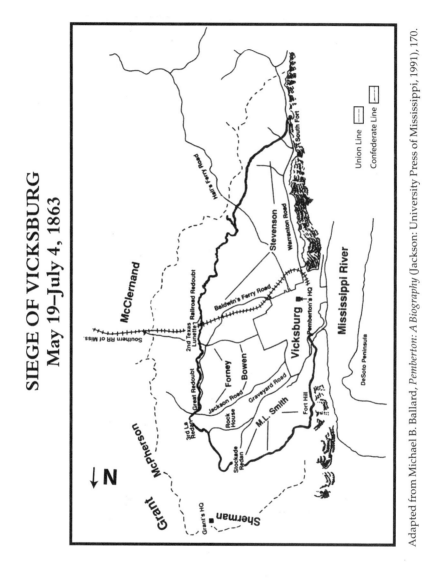

SIEGE OF VICKSBURG
May 19–July 4, 1863

Adapted from Michael B. Ballard, *Pemberton: A Biography* (Jackson: University Press of Mississippi, 1991), 170.

sider their shrinking food supply. Grant could not know how long all this might take, but unless something went horribly wrong to the rear, he thought surrender should be just a matter of time.[12]

Yet he still seemed overly concerned about Joseph Johnston. Even though Johnston had neither shown any inclination to fight at Jackson nor made any effort to move southwest from Canton to link with Pemberton before the fight at Champion Hill, Grant wanted this only viable Confederate menace on the horizon neutralized. Like any commander who had grown into his job, Grant hated loose ends, the kind that had come back to haunt him earlier in the war. Johnston must be considered a threat until Grant made sure he was not. If Johnston did come, Grant decided, he would find the going tough. As more men poured into the Union ranks, an impressive line of defensive works stretched from the Yazoo bluffs east and southeast to the Big Black crossings. Moreover, Grant sent patrols to gather information on Johnston's activities, and these detachments did their best to clean out the regions they visited of any food that might otherwise find its way into Rebel stomachs. Details also destroyed old Confederate earthworks east of the Big Black and tore up railroad tracks toward Jackson.[13]

On one occasion, Grant decided to accompany an expedition up the Yazoo to check exaggerated reports of a buildup of Johnston's forces. On the boat, Grant became ill; in fact, he had not been feeling well before he boarded the steamer. The whole thing seemed understandable enough; many Union soldiers suffered in the Mississippi summer heat and swampy conditions around Vicksburg. Yet, long after the fact, the old issue of Grant's drinking became associated with the trip. A newspaperman named Sylvanus Cadwallader wrote after Grant's death that Grant had been drunk. Charles Dana, Stanton's spy on the scene, who was traveling with the general, denied that Cadwallader had even been present, but Dana and James Wilson, one of Grant's aides who had no great fondness for his boss, alleged after the war that Grant *was* drunk on another river trip. This kind of assault on a famous person has not been rare in American history, and there is little evidence to prove or disprove the truth of either claim. What it did demonstrate was that once a public personality had any kind of label hung upon him, it was difficult to shake it off. Even if the story was accurate, it was equally true that Grant never let drinking get in the way of his goal of taking Vicksburg, nor in the way of any of his campaigns.[14]

Despite his illness, whatever its cause, Grant understood quickly enough that the reports regarding Johnston were false. There had been no signs of any Confederate concentration, and whatever Johnston might intend to do, there was little indication that he was yet doing it. Grant therefore turned his attention to other potential trouble spots, Young's Point and Milliken's Bend, for Rebel troops in Louisiana occasionally showed signs of aggression around Union supply depots on that side of the river. On June 7, black Union troops, assisted by the navy, fought off an attack at Milliken's Bend by John Walker's Confederate division. Rebel pressure on the Louisiana side of the river provided little relief for Pemberton's army, because the Union navy ruled the waters. Still, until the city surrendered, Grant felt anxious about his supply bases.[15]

As time went on, Grant's troop strength became formidable indeed. Halleck sent out calls for men to Ambrose Burnside, commanding the Department of the Ohio, to John Schofield, who headed the Department of the Missouri, and to Rosecrans in Tennessee. Rosecrans refused, since he was gearing up for operations against Braxton Bragg, but Schofield promised eight regiments, and Burnside sent some 8,000 men, designated the IX Corps. The extra manpower meant that Grant could rotate his men in and out of the siege lines, giving him a distinct advantage over Pemberton, whose trapped and thinly stretched army had little opportunity for relief.

Because he did not badger Washington about reinforcements with the same fervor as other Union generals, such as McClellan and Rosecrans, Grant probably received more attention. Yet displaying an attitude reminiscent of his pre-northern Mississippi invasion days, he could never believe there were enough, primarily because he still had so few facts about Johnston's activities. His manpower concerns had no foundation, for Johnston certainly had no ambition to attack Grant's lines. But Grant could not be sure, so he sent word to Stephen Hurlbut to keep the fewest men he could get by with in Memphis and send the rest to Vicksburg; he even said that giving up certain points in Kentucky and West Tennessee would be permissible. Hurlbut, shocked at orders that would strip his area to bare bones, appealed directly to Halleck, who diplomatically assured him that he could retain the troops essential to the security of the Memphis area.[16]

When a Confederate cavalry patrol skirmished with Union riders west of the Big Black on June 22, Grant decided that Johnston must be moving. He quickly ordered Sherman to send two brigades from his XV Corps and three more from Mcpherson's XVII Corps to the Big Black to repulse Johnston. Soon some 34,000 men and seventy-two cannon were deployed along the Big Black's western bluffs, but Johnston did not come. Grant knew, however, that unless Johnston abandoned Mississippi and took his forces elsewhere, he must be dealt with sooner or later, so he kept his forces in place, poised to go after Johnston when the time came.[17]

Meanwhile, the siege drifted inexorably to its climax. Union engineers set off explosives planted under Confederate works at the Third Louisiana Redan on June 25. The event resulted in a significant gap in Pemberton's lines, but Union troops rushing into the crater created by the blast were shot down in hordes. Though the assault failed, Pemberton's forces in the area were stunned by the extent of the explosion, and the Federals moved ever closer to Rebel lines in that sector. A follow-up explosion on July 1 in the same area did even more damage, though this time Union officers were smart enough not to send their men into another trap.[18]

The explosions seemed to portend the end for Pemberton's hungry, bedraggled army. The Confederates still had large, but shrinking, stores of food, but Pemberton's policy of reducing rations to stretch provisions and thus prolong the siege had taken a heavy toll on the health of his men. Finally, having heard nothing from Johnston for some time and seeing no other choice, Pemberton decided he must surrender and sent word that he thought Johnston should open negotiations. Johnston refused, for to do so, he argued, "would be a confession of weakness on my part." Pemberton hoped that Grant might be willing to let the Vicksburg army go in peace as long as the city was surrendered, but Johnston knew better. Johnston's attitude was simple: Pemberton had gotten himself boxed in, and he would have to suffer the consequences.[19]

On July 3, Grant received a note from Pemberton requesting an armistice to discuss the surrender of Vicksburg and proposing that he and Grant each name three commissioners to negotiate terms. John Bowen, who had known Grant before the war, delivered the message. Grant immediately responded, as he had at Fort Donelson, that he would consider no terms except the unconditional surrender of the city and Pemberton's army. He assured Pemberton that he appreciated the Confederates' determination and bravery and would see to it that as prisoners they would be treated appropriately. In response to an inquiry from Bowen, Grant said that he would be willing to meet with Pemberton in front of McPherson's corps at 3:00 P.M.

Bowen used the meeting time to mislead Pemberton into thinking that Grant had asked for the conference and was willing to negotiate. Grant intended no such thing, so when the two men and their escorts met that afternoon, there was much embarrassment over the misunderstanding. Bowen's thinking seemed to have been that if he could get the two commanding generals together, something would be worked out. When Grant made clear that he had not asked to negotiate anything, an irritated Pemberton assured him that many more Federal soldiers would be buried before the Union army marched into Vicksburg.

At this point, Bowen, sensing that an opportunity was about to be lost, suggested that the two generals step aside and allow their representatives to discuss the matter. Pemberton later claimed that this was Grant's idea, but Grant insisted that it was Bowen's; in any event, by assenting, Grant in effect acceded to an earlier Pemberton suggestion that commissioners negotiate terms. Grant refused, however, to agree to the proposals that resulted, which included allowing Pemberton's army to march out of Vicksburg fully armed, with colors and field batteries, while the Union army would march into the city and retain the siege guns and small arms left behind. Pemberton then asked Grant to present his parameters again.

Considering his terms, Grant called his officers together to share with them the substance of the meeting and to hear their suggestions. (He denied, as Pemberton later implied, that it was akin to a council of war, but he did say it was the closest he ever came to holding such a meeting.) How much his subordinates participated in putting together the final proposal is not totally clear. Grant did back away from unconditional surrender but insisted in his memoirs that his final draft was not favored by most of his officers; whatever history might say, Grant wanted to make it clear that he, not a committee, made the terms.

He decided the prudent thing to do was to parole Pemberton's army: that is, to have each soldier sign an agreement not to get back into the war until exchanged on a one-to-one basis with prisoners held by Confederate forces. This would more quickly free up much of Grant's army to go to other theaters and campaigns. Upon completion of the signing of paroles, Grant would permit the Confederates to march out of the city. Pemberton agreed, and the surrender was done. Specifically, Confederate officers kept their sidearms and clothing, and the field, staff, and cavalry officers were allowed one horse each. Soldiers in the ranks retained their clothes but no other property. Rations and thirty wagons for transporting supplies were issued to the parolees.[20]

While Union guns fired salutes of celebration and his soldiers cheered, Grant sent a brief, to-the-point message to Halleck: "The enemy surrendered this morning. The only terms allowed is their parole as prisoners of war." He explained why he had chosen the parole option, reported that Sherman would soon begin chasing after Johnston, and promised that troops would be sent to help Banks as soon as possible and that the IX Corps would be returned to Burnside (although in fact Grant retained the IX Corps for a time, assigning it to Sherman). While Sherman sought Johnston, McPherson would see to the specifics of the surrender, especially the red tape of paroling prisoners and trying to return Vicksburg to some sense of normalcy as a functioning town. McPherson was ultimately placed in command of the Vicksburg area.[21]

As news of the surrender spread across the North, Grant once more became a hero, this time gaining even more fame than at Donelson. His victory came on the heels of Robert E. Lee's defeat on July 3 at Gettysburg, and as more news drifted in across the country, it quickly became obvious that Grant's triumph had been much more complete and substantial than the Union success in Pennsylvania. Although he enjoyed the high of achieving a goal so long sought, Grant no doubt wondered what would come next. He had some ideas about future campaigning, but for the time being he had to attend to various details involved in the aftermath of winning.

While he reviewed policies for the military occupation of Vicksburg, Grant had an interesting encounter with Pemberton before the Confederate commander left the city. One day he stopped at a home where Pemberton and his staff had congregated, perhaps hoping for a kind of West Point reunion, but the Confederates treated the Federal conquerors quite icily. Fred Grant, the general's son, wondered if these men realized that his father had respectfully ordered the celebratory firing of guns to cease following the surrender; he had shown more regard for his foes than they seemed prepared to show him. Of course, Grant could afford to be magnanimous. The little episode says more than that, however. Grant obviously did not come away from the surrender in an arrogant mood. Having been through a lot and endured much to get to this point, he certainly understood that a general's fame and reputation were only as good as his next campaign.[22]

Meanwhile, more good news came in. Union troops had repulsed a Confederate attack on Helena on July 4, and Sherman, after besieging Jackson for about a week, had chased Johnston into central Mississippi. Given the hot weather and water shortages, Sherman decided to let the Confederates go, judging correctly that they would no longer be a threat to Vicksburg. News from downriver indicated that Banks had at last taken Port Hudson, which was surrendered on July 9; Grant's victory had made that Confederate fortress untenable.[23]

All the good news turned a bit sour when Grant watched his army being broken up to provide reinforcements elsewhere, especially to Rosecrans in Tennessee. Grant had made clear to Washington that he thought Mobile should be his next target and hoped to take his Vicksburg army there to get the job done. In the meantime, while his soldiers rested, Grant asked to visit New Orleans, where he would begin making operational plans for the Mobile campaign. But Halleck rejected both the proposals and the trip, and Grant reflected in his memoirs, "So far as my experience with General Halleck went it was very much easier for him to refuse a favor than to grant one." He therefore gritted his teeth and sent some 4,000 men to Banks for further campaigning in Louisiana, the IX Corps to Kentucky, and 5,000 soldiers to Missouri to help thwart the activities of Sterling Price. Another brigade left for Natchez to garrison that town. Troops still at Vicksburg occasionally went after Rebel raiders and guerrillas who were causing trouble on both sides of the Mississippi. The first week of August, Grant sent additional troops—McClernand's old command, the XIII Corps—to Banks. After visiting with Banks, Grant concluded that Banks's plans would accomplish little, and the only memorable thing about their meeting occurred when a horse Grant was riding spooked and "probably fell on me," as he later recalled in the fog of memory caused by the accident. With his body severely swollen from being mashed under the weight of the animal, Grant spent several weeks in extreme pain, recuperating in New Orleans and later back at Vicksburg. Predictably, his fall fueled additional unfounded rumors about his drinking.[24]

Following so closely on the euphoria of victory at Vicksburg, the lack of action thereafter must have been a terrible disappointment to Grant, especially since he had to split up his army to support campaigning that seemed minor compared to his capture of the city. A laudatory note from Abraham Lincoln helped ease his restlessness: "When you got below, and took Port-Gibson, Grand Gulf, and vicinity, I thought you should go down the river and join Gen. Banks; and when you turned Northward East of the Big Black, I feared it was a mistake. I now wish to make the personal acknowledgment that you were right, and I was wrong." Lincoln went on to explain why the decision had been made to forgo Grant's hoped-for campaign against Mobile. France's presence in Mexico had fueled concerns for the safety of western Texas; hence that area and others were higher priorities at the moment.[25]

Lincoln's explanation was enough for Grant; though he disagreed with Lincoln's strategic decision, he no doubt appreciated the president's generous congratulations. It was his habit, if not satisfied, to accept whatever came next and move on; that mindset, which came naturally, had served him well. Grant had come a long way from Belmont. He had learned from mistakes, and he had repeated mistakes. He had struggled to acquire a good feel for the politics of command, even though he still found it all distasteful. He had experienced the highs and lows: he had formulated plans that failed and some that worked; he had used his commanders well at times and not so effectively at others. In short, Grant had grown into his job as all initially inexperienced army commanders must if they are to succeed. He had seemingly reached his personal pinnacle on the heights of Vicksburg. But the war was not yet won, and a man with Grant's credentials surely had more to do before peace reigned. He had no idea just how much work remained.

NOTES

1. Grant, *Memoirs*, 355; Simpson, *Grant*, 209.
2. Bearss, *Vicksburg*, 2:753–73.
3. Grant, *Memoirs*, 355.
4. Ibid.; *OR*, ser. 1, vol. 24, pt. 1, pp. 54–55, 756; Bearss, *Vicksburg*, 3:807–8.
5. *OR*, ser. 1, vol. 24, pt. 3, pp. 331–32.
6. Ibid., pt. 1, pp. 55–56, 172–73; Bearss, *Vicksburg*, 2:835–61.
7. Grant, *Memoirs*, 356.
8. Ibid.; Bearss, *Vicksburg*, 2:858.
9. *OR*, ser. 1, vol. 24, pt. 3, p. 914; pt. 1, pp. 276–77.

10. Grant, *Memoirs*, 360.

11. Ibid.; *OR*, ser. 1, vol. 24, pt. 1, pp. 43, 84, 102–3, 159–70; pt. 3, pp. 351, 419; Kiper, *McClernand*, 268–78.

12. Grant, *Memoirs*, 363.

13. Ibid., 363, 365; *OR*, ser. 1, vol. 24, pt. 2, pp. 171–74.

14. *OR*, ser. 1, vol. 24, pt. 3, p. 387; Charles A. Dana, *Recollections of the Civil War* (New York, 1898, 1902), 82–83; Simpson, *Grant*, 207–8.

15. Grant, *Memoirs*, 366. On the Milliken's Bend battle see Bearss, *Vicksburg*, 3:1153–1204 passim.

16. *OR*, ser. 1, vol. 24, pt. 3, pp. 368–69, 376–77, 381–84, 386.

17. Ibid., pt. 2, pp. 245–46; pt. 3, pp. 427–28, 430–31, 439, 449.

18. Grant, *Memoirs*, 369–70.

19. Ballard, *Pemberton*, 177.

20. *OR*, ser. 1, vol. 24, pt. 1, pp. 281–84; pt. 3, pp. 982–83; John C. Pemberton, "The Terms of Surrender," in Johnson and Buell, *Battles and Leaders of the Civil War*, 3:544; Grant, *Memoirs*, 374–78.

21. Grant, *Memoirs*, 381, 387; *OR*, ser. 1, vol. 24, pt. 3, pp. 478, 481, 484.

22. Fred Grant, "General Grant," *National Tribune*, February 10, 1887.

23. Bearss, *Vicksburg*, 3:1207–41. On Jackson see Edwin C. Bearss, *The Siege of Jackson, July 10–17* (Baltimore, MD, 1981).

24. Grant, *Memoirs*, 388–90; Simpson, *Grant*, 223.

25. Basler, *Lincoln*, 6:326, 374.

CHAPTER ELEVEN

CHATTANOOGA AND ANOTHER SIEGE

WHILE STILL RECUPERATING from his riding mishap, Grant received urgent telegrams from Henry Halleck requesting troops for the Chattanooga area, where William Rosecrans was locked in a campaign against Braxton Bragg. Grant managed to start Sherman's XV Corps, less one division left with Mcpherson in Vicksburg, plus a division in exchange from Mcpherson's XVII Corps (already en route to Memphis), on the long trip to Chattanooga. Halleck wanted someone, preferably Sherman or Mcpherson, to take charge of these four divisions, and Grant sent Sherman to command what was still designated the Army of the Tennessee. Frank Blair replaced Sherman as head of the XV Corps. While messages flew back and forth, Bragg's army routed Rosecrans's forces at the Battle of Chickamauga, September 19–20, 1863, and Rosecrans retreated into Chattanooga. Grant later wrote of the resulting consternation in Washington: "The administration as well as the General-in-chief was nearly frantic at the situation of affairs there."[1]

Meanwhile, Halleck ordered Grant to travel upriver to Cairo, Illinois, as soon as his health permitted. Though still quite stiff and sore from his fall, Grant started at once, arriving in Columbus, Kentucky, on October 16. From there he went on to Cairo, where he was instructed to go via Indianapolis to Louisville for a meeting at the Galt House hotel with a War Department representative. At Indianapolis, however, Grant met with Secretary of War Edwin Stanton, finding himself for the first time in the company of the man with whom he had previously communicated only via telegraph. When Stanton entered the railroad car where Grant sat with his staff, the secretary, likewise having never seen the general, assumed that Grant's medical director was Grant. The slightly embarrassing though amusing moment passed, and Stanton, along with Governor John Brough of Ohio, rode the train with Grant to Louisville. Grant must have known at once that the government had something important for him to do, or Stanton would not have come to see him personally.[2]

Other than a cryptic message from Halleck that he should continue to Nashville, when able, and take command of troops being sent to Rosecrans, Grant had no inkling as to his future. Rumors of being sent east to command the Army of the Potomac had not thrilled him; he preferred to remain with soldiers and generals he had come to know in the West. As the train clicked along, Stanton got to the point. He had two sets of orders, both creating the Military Division of the Mississippi, composed of the Departments of the Cumberland, the Ohio, and the Tennessee plus all territory west of the Alleghenies to the Mississippi and north of Banks's dominion in the Southwest. The difference between the two sets was that one left current departmental commanders in place; the other removed Rosecrans in favor of George Thomas. But both placed Grant in overall charge of the division, and he, no doubt recalling his harsh relationship with Rosecrans in Mississippi as well as Rosecrans's less than spectacular record in Tennessee, immediately chose the latter.

By the time the train chugged into Louisville, everything had been settled. Grant spent October 18 listening to Stanton's review of the military situation from the War Department's perspective. At the end of the day, Grant recalled, "All matters of discussion seemed exhausted, and I left the hotel to spend the evening" with his wife, Julia, who was traveling with him, as she did whenever possible. Grant learned later that Stanton had received a message from Charles Dana, now in Chattanooga, to the effect that Rosecrans was about to abandon the city; Dana advised Stanton to stop the evacuation.[3]

The current situation in Chattanooga had evolved from curious beginnings dating back to August 16. At that point, after urgings and threats from Washington, Rosecrans had finally begun a campaign against Bragg, skillfully maneuvering the Confederates from Tennessee into northwest Georgia. Then Bragg had suddenly turned and attacked Rosecrans's forces at a time when they were widely spread out and therefore vulnerable. Grant understood that during the spring and summer his campaign at Vicksburg had forced the Confederates to send help to Mississippi from Bragg. With Bragg thus weakened, Rosecrans had a wonderful opportunity to advance, and he did push forward in the Tullahoma campaign, beginning in late June, yet his campaign was one of maneuver, not battles. Bragg did not get reinforcements from Mississippi until after Joseph Johnston evacuated Jackson for a second time, when he was reinforced by Johnston's troops, plus some of Pemberton's old army, and, most significantly, James Longstreet's corps from Robert E. Lee's Army of Northern Virginia. With this considerably larger army, Bragg had become aggressive and soundly whipped Rosecrans along Chickamauga Creek south of Chattanooga.

Rosecrans's retreat into Chattanooga had created both strategic and logistical problems. Any move farther north meant that a key city, not to mention valuable munitions, would have to be abandoned. Rosecrans's railroad supply line, which ran northwest to Nashville, was subject to Confederate control where it crossed the Tennessee River at Bridgeport, Alabama. Moreover, the good roads from Chattanooga to Bridgeport were vulnerable to Bragg's artillery fire from positions on Lookout and Raccoon Mountains west of Chattanooga. A withdrawal would not only cost the Union forces Chattanooga but would also open Rosecrans's battered army to attack and pursuit. His men and animals were lacking just about every necessity, and demoralization was widespread. Such was the mess U. S. Grant had to salvage.[4]

Grant's reaction mirrored the high confidence level that victory at Vicksburg had produced. The intervening days and months had been trying, both physically and mentally, but at last sensing action again, he charged into his new job just as he expected his men to charge the enemy. First, he wrote an order assuming command of the Military Division of the Mississippi, and then he sent word to Rosecrans that Thomas was replacing him as leader of the Army of the Cumberland. Another message told Thomas that Chattanooga must be held "at all hazards." Thomas, with a new job and a new boss, wasted no time in responding that the army would stay in Chattanooga until it starved, if necessary.[5]

On October 20, Grant and his staff headed south to Chattanooga, stopping overnight in Nashville. There he had to endure the long, tedious speech of another politician, this time Andrew Johnson, future vice president and president, and Grant "was in torture while he was delivering it." This aspect of celebrity did not please the general, but by now he recognized it as part of the game he had to play in order to survive. Grant himself was not a speechmaker; in fact, he dreaded the thought of becoming one, unaware of what the future held. Fortunately, on this occasion, he did not have to make public remarks.[6]

In Nashville, Grant wired Ambrose Burnside, who commanded a corps then occupying Knoxville in East Tennessee, to see to it that the least number of men necessary be assigned to garrison key points in his area. Another message went to David Porter, then at Cairo, requesting him to make sure that rations, then on their way east by boat from St. Louis, were protected and delivered via the Tennessee at points west of Chattanooga for Sherman and his troops. Thomas received orders to send men to improve a wagon road that connected Chattanooga and Bridgeport.

On the twenty-first, Grant journeyed farther south. Arriving in Stevenson, Alabama, that night, he met with Rosecrans, who was traveling north. Grant thought his former subordinate from the Iuka-Corinth operations gave a good report and offered good suggestions; he could not help wondering why Rosencrans had done nothing with them. After that meeting, Grant and his party went on to the terminus of the railroad at Bridgeport and spent the night.[7]

Next day, the entourage rode over high hills to Chattanooga. Some portions of the roadways were so steep that Grant, in his still debilitated condition, had to be carried. What the men fresh from victory in Mississippi saw along the road was overwhelming. Grant was stunned to find hundreds of broken and scattered wagons and even more shocked by the sight and stench of the "carcasses of thousands of starved mules and horses." Obviously, the situation was even worse than he had been told. Along the way he sent another message ordering Burnside to secure additional rounds for his artillery and small arms. Grant had in mind using Burnside's troops to help break the Confederate blockade of Chattanooga.[8]

At last the weary general reached Thomas's headquarters, which he shared until his staff could set up his own. Thomas greeted the new commander quite coolly; perhaps he resented this interloper, who seemed to take over in a rather heavy-handed manner. Thomas, a native Virginian who had decided to fight with the Union, may have been a bit paranoid about the influence and power of his fellow generals. During the post-Shiloh campaign against Corinth, Thomas must have felt manipulated by Halleck when he was given command of four of Grant's old divisions, and then, once Grant resumed commanding the Army of the Tennessee, had been returned to the command of his single division. Having been a part of the Army of the Ohio, Thomas may also have sided with Don Carlos Buell, who had had a tense relationship with Grant. Or perhaps jealousy was a factor. Whatever the case, Thomas was clearly not overjoyed to see Grant.

As other generals made a point of coming by to pay their respects, Grant learned more about the strategic situation. None of them, of course, admitted to having supported Rosecrans's plan to withdraw, since they all knew that Thomas had been ordered to stay put. Grant's most beneficial visitor turned out to be General W. F. Smith, chief engineer of the Army of the Cumberland, who, Grant recalled, "explained the situation of the two armies and the topography of the country so plainly that I could see it without an inspection." Out of sight of the Confederate guns, Smith already had set up a sawmill and was instructing men in bridge construction. Grant liked what he heard. Plans could now be formulated to remedy the Union forces' previously bleak situation, and to further enhance his optimism, Grant asked for and received permission to place Sherman in command of the Army of the Tennessee permanently. Soon, Grant would have the most trusted member of his Vicksburg team with him, plus Sherman's corps and a division from McPherson, to participate in the Chattanooga operations. These Vicksburg veterans would now find themselves in the position of breaking a siege instead of conducting one.[9]

Although Smith had described the lay of the land, Grant knew he needed to see as much of it as he could for himself. So on October 24, accompanied by a portion of his staff plus Smith and Thomas, he explored the Tennessee's course, which twisted west and south from Chattanooga. They stopped at Brown's Ferry, a few miles below Lookout Mountain, the eminence overlooking Chattanooga and then occupied by Confederates. Across the way, Rebel pickets who saw this group of blue-clad riders chose to ignore them rather than open fire. Grant remarked rather laconically, "I suppose they looked upon the garrison of Chattanooga as prisoners of war, feeding or starving themselves, and thought it would be inhuman to kill any of them except in self-defence."[10]

Grant's immediate solution to the army's serious supply problem was to set up what the soldiers soon dubbed the "cracker line." As Grant became more familiar with the area, he realized the scope of the problem caused by Rosecrans's retreat. Bragg, following close behind, had tremendous geographic advantages that allowed him to pen up the larger Union army, for Chattanooga sat in a valley, bound on the east by Missionary Ridge and on the west by Lookout Mountain. The Memphis & Charleston Railroad coming east from Memphis entered the city along the base of Lookout Mountain, between the mountain and the Tennessee River. Smaller streams flowed east of Missionary Ridge and west of Lookout Mountain. To the west of Lookout Mountain stood Raccoon Mountain.

Bragg had entrenched his army from the northernmost reach of Missionary Ridge, across the ridge, and across the southern approaches to Chattanooga; other defenses were scattered about on Lookout and Raccoon Mountains as well as on low land west of the town. North of Chattanooga, Confederate cavalry provided a threat to any Union attempt to bring wagonloads of supplies from that direction, and the steep terrain and multiple streams would make treacherous any Federal effort to retreat north. Further, the only railroads that provided hope of succor from the west or northwest would be vulnerable to Bragg's guns long before supply trains could enter the city.[11] The cracker or, more correctly, the supply line that Grant envisioned necessitated setting up a route from Bridgeport to Chattanooga that would be safe from Bragg's interference. The concept was clear and obvious, but making it happen required careful planning, and much depended on Smith's being able to put bridging equipment together and get it down the Tennessee without letting the Confederates see what was going on.

Halleck had sent reinforcements to Rosecrans from the XI and XII Corps of the Army of the Potomac by a circuitous rail route, but their presence in Chattanooga would have only exacerbated the supply problem. Thomas therefore ordered them to stop and camp at Bridgeport, located out of Bragg's range to the west, where trains from Nashville could bring them food. Now the plan consisted first of having Joseph Hooker, commanding the contingent from the eastern theater, cross his troops to the east bank of the Tennessee at Bridgeport and then march behind Raccoon Mountain along the railroad via Whiteside and Wauhatchie to Brown's Ferry, located west of Chattanooga on the Tennessee where the river flowed back north after curving in front of Lookout Mountain. A division of the Army of the Cumberland was ordered to move down the Tennessee's north bank via a little-used road, then cross the river behind Hooker to guard the road against any Rebel attempts to approach Hooker's rear.

While all this went on, engineer Smith received a command of 4,000 men, detached for special service, and sent 1,800 at night to carry some sixty pontoons to a point on the Tennessee where they could be put into the stream and guided downriver past enemy troops along the base of Lookout Mountain. These men would land the equipment at Brown's Ferry on the west bank and chase away any Confederates in the area. Once Brown's Ferry was secure, a road that stretched west by southwest to Kelley's Ferry above Bridgeport would be open. Supplies could be unloaded safely from transports at Kelley's Ferry and carried by wagon to Brown's, then across the Tennessee and into Chattanooga. Meanwhile, Smith took the remainder of his force along the north-northeast bank of the Tennessee to Brown's Ferry with the additional material needed to build a bridge. Their route would not be visible from the top of Lookout Mountain. If Confederate observers there thought they could watch all enemy movements, they were about to learn differently.

Everything went pretty much according to plan. Hooker crossed at Bridgeport on October 26. The detachment taking the pontoons downstream left around 3:00 A.M. the morning of the twenty-seventh, and Smith's ground troops began their march to rendezvous with the pontoons. The river wing of the operation landed and overwhelmed the few Rebel pickets in the area, and by 7:00 A.M., Smith's force commanded a hill that overlooked Brown's Ferry. While some men worked to lay the bridge, others dug in to defend the place against any enemy forces that might appear. The bridge detail completed its work by 10:00 A.M., and everything seemed to be in place for a supply line connecting Chattanooga and Bridgeport. When Hooker finished his march, the job was done, for his men now deployed to cut off enemy pickets downriver from Brown's Ferry to Bridgeport. Federal troops repulsed Confederate attempts to disrupt the Union cordon. With men in place to defend the land route from Bridgeport to Brown's Ferry, and a safe route from ferry to ferry, Grant's soldiers soon had the cracker line in business. On October 30 a steamboat delivered supplies to Kelley's Ferry, and food wound its way to hungry Union soldiers.[12]

Grant's strategy had been effective because it had been simple. No complicated marches were required, and the terrain that seemed to be so pro-Confederate in fact told Grant exactly what he could and could not do to set up the supply line. Of course, as in the Vicksburg campaign, he was helped by having an opponent whose idea of aggression was usually to sit and do nothing. Bragg had not reevaluated his army's position on his left, and so he did not understand that he was vulnerable there, surprisingly and almost humorously vulnerable. Since his strained relations with his commanders had only been worsened by James Longstreet's arrival in north Georgia, Bragg made a decision that he hoped would relieve the personality conflicts and help him recapture whatever momentum he had after Chickamauga. He sent Longstreet to attack Burnside at Knoxville.

Longstreet's departure placed great pressure on Grant, for he understood the Lincoln administration's emphasis on keeping East Tennessee secure for the Union. Many vocal pro-Unionists lived in the region, and Burnside's presence there was important to Lincoln, perhaps symbolically more than militarily. If Longstreet managed to whip Burnside, the ramifications would be enormous, and Grant knew that he must prevent such a catastrophe, or people in the North would forget the cracker line very quickly. Grant had no way of knowing that Longstreet, whose notoriety as one of Robert E. Lee's stalwarts in the Virginia theater of war had been well earned, had made his reputation while serving under Lee, and that the Knoxville campaign would prove him better suited to be a subordinate than to exercise independent command. But Grant had to act quickly and without consideration of possible enemy mistakes. Grant appreciated the fact that Burnside's condition was "desperate," but at least he was not yet besieged. Although supplies in East Tennessee were not plentiful, Burnside faced nothing like the situation that had haunted Rosecrans. Grant realized that he could not tarry for long, however; his war thus far had demonstrated all too well how quickly the fortunes of command could change.[13]

Grant's first order of business, once supplies were flowing, was obvious to him: he must get his trusted friend Sherman quickly to Chattanooga. Grant ordered Sherman to cease repairing the Memphis & Charleston Railroad as his army marched, in order to speed his arrival to the front, though he did tell Sherman to send a detachment to repair and keep open a branch line that led from Decatur to Nashville. Doing so would provide two routes from Nashville, to north-northeast Alabama and into Chattanooga, thus easing supply route congestion, especially if Grant had to provision not only his own forces in Chattanooga but also Burnside's in Knoxville. Sherman later benefited from this insightful logistical move when he invaded Georgia. Grant certainly had learned the value of secure supply and communications routes, and he continued putting those lessons to good use.[14]

Longstreet left for Knoxville on November 4, and Grant, still waiting for Sherman but under heavy pressure from Washington

George Thomas. From Ezra J. Warner, *Generals in Blue: Lives of the Union Command-ers* (Baton Rouge: Louisiana State University Press, 1964), 500.

to help Burnside, reacted quickly. Since sending troops to Burnside would solve nothing and only exacerbate the supply situation at Knoxville, Grant made the only move he thought logical under the circumstances: he ordered Thomas to attack Bragg's right, hoping that pressure on the Confederate flank would force Bragg to recall Longstreet.

Thomas produced many reasons why he could not make such an attack, some of them quite legitimate, but his recalcitrance either opened old wounds or created a new breach between him and Grant that never completely healed. Grant liked commanders who did, or at least made an effort to do, what circumstances dictated, but Thomas was the sort who would not move unless he felt completely prepared. Thomas may well have been influenced by his recently departed commander, Rosecrans, who had acted similarly in Tennessee in the spring of 1863 when immediate action could have helped Grant at Vicksburg. Grant must have wondered whether Thomas would turn out to be another Rosecrans. In any event, Grant notified Washington that he could do nothing more until Sherman arrived, and he sent a message urging Burnside to hold on as best he could.

Burnside seemingly did not worry about Longstreet; in fact, he suggested to Grant that evacuating positions south and west of Knoxville would pull Longstreet farther from Chattanooga, thereby causing the Confederates logistical problems. Grant agreed: "If you can hold Longstreet in check until [Sherman, then at Bridgeport] gets up, or by skirmishing and falling back can avoid serious loss to yourself and gain time, I will be able to force the enemy back from here and place a force between Longstreet and Bragg that must inevitably make the former take to the mountain-passes by every available road, to get to his supplies."[15]

As Sherman's troops marched into the Chattanooga area, shielded by hills north of town from Bragg's observers, Grant refined his offensive plans. He ordered Sherman to move into place on Bragg's right and attack up the north slopes of Missionary Ridge. Thomas's target would also be Missionary Ridge in cooperation with Sherman's advance, while Hooker attacked the Rebel left and cleared the enemy off Lookout Mountain. On November 18, Grant detailed his expectations to Thomas:

> You will co-operate with Sherman. The troops in Chattanooga Valley should be well concentrated on your left flank, leaving only the necessary force to defend fortifications on the right and center, and a movable column of one division in readiness to move wherever ordered. This division should show itself as threateningly as possible on the most practicable line for making an attack up the valley. Your effort then will be to form a junction with Sherman, making your advance well towards the northern end

of Missionary Ridge, and moving as near simultaneously with him as possible.

While Thomas worked with Sherman, Hooker should be able to carry out his mission of getting past Lookout Mountain and hitting Bragg's left. As Grant noted, these operations would negate Hooker's need to protect the supply route area, for Bragg could not send troops west while being pressured all along his line.[16]

Meanwhile, Longstreet made contact with Burnside at Knoxville. Grant knew that but nothing more, for Longstreet's position between Burnside and Chattanooga cut off Grant's communications from Knoxville. He later recalled worries over Burnside's unknown situation: "The President, the Secretary of War, and General Halleck, were in an agony of suspense. My suspense was also great, but more endurable, because I was where I could soon do something to relieve the situation." Rain frustrated his efforts, however, holding up Sherman's deployment for an attack.[17]

On November 22, Grant learned from a Rebel prisoner that Bragg was sending more troops to Longstreet. Grant deduced the obvious: Bragg had decided to gamble that he could, by sending reinforcements, help Longstreet dispatch Burnside, and then recall the same troops to take care of Grant. Though he had planned to launch his offensive on the twenty-fourth, weather permitting, Grant now decided to send Thomas's Army of the Cumberland on a reconnaissance in force a day early against a strong position called Orchard Knob, anchored by Fort Wood, between modern-day downtown Chattanooga and Missionary Ridge. He hoped that this limited offensive would scare Bragg into recalling some of his troops and, beyond that, permit Thomas to get into a better position to attack in conjunction with Sherman the next day.

Thomas's men performed well, driving Confederates from Orchard Knob back to entrenchments along the base of Missionary Ridge. The fighting was heavy, but Thomas outnumbered the enemy, and after chasing Bragg's troops back from their advanced position, the Army of the Cumberland occupied Rebel trenches, facing to the reverse side against the former occupants. Grant's plan worked beautifully, for Bragg immediately rushed messengers to the railroad station and recalled the troops about to leave for Longstreet's front. Now that he had Bragg's attention, Grant continued preparing for major assaults on the twenty-fourth.[18]

During the night of the twenty-third, Sherman was still battling high water on the Tennessee and North and South Chickamauga Creeks, which had to be negotiated before he deployed for his attack on Missionary Ridge. Peter Osterhaus's division lagged behind, waiting for the churning Tennessee to settle down before crossing at Brown's Ferry, for the pontoon bridge there had been washed away. Grant ordered that division to join Hooker rather than hold up Sherman any further. Sherman displayed little aggression during his deployment efforts; his advance did not begin crossing the Tennessee until around 2:00 A.M. and did not deploy for the attack until noon of the twenty-fourth. Not until the next morning did he learn that he was not at the north slope of Missionary Ridge proper: when his front line brushed aside Rebel skirmishers, he discovered a large gap between them and the real north end of the ridge—and there they discovered Pat Cleburne's division, Bragg's best. Sherman had a fight on his hands, and he must have thought back to Chickasaw Bayou, not quite a year earlier, when he had slammed into a wall of well-fortified resistance. Meanwhile, Thomas, having made his move a day earlier, had his troops spend the twenty-fourth strengthening his position. The spotlight of the fighting shifted southwest to Hooker.[19]

With one of Sherman's divisions joining his two, Hooker had a formidable force to carry out his mission of clearing Lookout Mountain of Confederates and preying upon Bragg's left flank. He did as instructed, his troops driving the Confederates relentlessly in what became known as the "battle above the clouds," for low clouds and mist enshrouded the upper reaches of the mountain, and though sounds of battle could be heard from below, no one could see what was going on. Carter Stevenson, the same general whose division had been battered at Champion Hill, evacuated his position per Bragg's orders and fell back all the way up Missionary Ridge to a position behind the line on the Confederate right. By the next morning, Hooker had sealed Lookout Mountain from Bragg and begun crossing Lookout Valley. Soon he would be in position to threaten Bragg's left along the southern reaches of Missionary Ridge.[20]

So far, everything had gone as Grant had hoped, with the exception that Sherman was still feeling his way. Sherman and Grant, convinced by light Confederate opposition on Sherman's front that a decisive charge could run the Confederates off Missionary Ridge, had not known that there was a split in the terrain of the ridge and

CHATTANOOGA
November 23–25, 1863

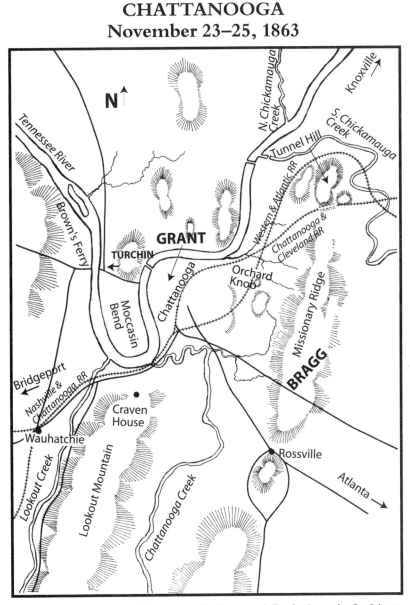

Adapted from James Lee McDonough, *Chattanooga: A Deathgrip on the Confederacy* (Knoxville: University of Tennessee Press, 1984), 80.

that across that divide, Pat Cleburne's division waited. Grant put a good face on the situation, reporting to Washington that Sherman had "carried the end of Missionary Ridge" (which was technically but only partially true) and that Hooker now controlled the eastern slope of Lookout Mountain. Lincoln telegraphed his congratulations but added, "Remember Burnside." Halleck, too, responded, "I fear that Burnside is hard pushed, and that any further delay may prove fatal. I know you will do all in your power to relieve him."[21]

November 25 dawned as a clear, spectacular, and decisive winter day. Grant sent an encouraging note to Burnside; Sherman prepared to attack; Hooker received instructions to advance and drive away any Rebels still between him and Bragg's left on Missionary Ridge. Thomas, meanwhile, would stay put until Hooker made contact with the southern end of Missionary Ridge. Sherman and Grant now understood that Sherman had not reached the main ridge and would have a harder time gaining a foothold there than originally supposed. Just as Sherman had faced Pemberton's best troops at Vicksburg during the May assaults, in Cleburne he was facing Bragg's best.

Action began early, with Sherman's veterans advancing under a hot fire. As the fighting ebbed and flowed, Bragg and then Grant provided reinforcements to their respective forces. Thomas sent a division, and Bragg—who, like many that day, could see everything unfolding in a grand panorama along the ridge and down in the valley—likewise sent more men to counter the Union buildup (though none of these actually became engaged in the fighting; Bragg's line broke in the face of Thomas's attack so the flow of action kept them out of the fight.) Grant watched too, and he kept looking anxiously for Hooker's arrival on Bragg's left, hoping to force the Confederates to shift enough troops in that direction to take pressure off Sherman. But hours went by as Hooker, delayed by high waters along Chattanooga Creek where the Confederates had burned a bridge, took longer than expected.[22] Grant, realizing he must do something else, told Thomas to send his remaining troops against the Confederate center. Again, Thomas's slow response angered his commander. When the charge did not get under way in a timely manner, Grant personally intervened, and soon a Union wave pushed against the base of Missionary Ridge.

Grant had intended these men only to push hard against advanced Confederate positions and then stop, re-form, and wait for further orders. He wanted to reassess his tactical options, but he never got the chance. When the assault overwhelmed the first Confederate line, the victorious Union soldiers, rather than stopping and waiting, kept right on going, soon smashing the line at the base of the ridge. Then they started climbing the heights, where another Confederate line awaited them about halfway up with still more at the top. The steep angle of the ridge wall from the crest to the valley below meant that Confederate artillery was useless, for the muzzles of the guns could not be depressed enough to fire with any effect against the Federals climbing and shooting. Bragg made the job easier, for by strengthening his right he had weakened his center. Rebel morale had already been damaged by the mere sight of Grant's army swarming like a huge bed of ants all along the valley from Sherman's position to the north to Hooker's troops at the south, and the Confederates watching heavy lines of infantry coming at them began to break from their positions and retreat on their own.

Grant, Thomas, and other officers watched spellbound as the Union wave ascended the heights of Missionary Ridge. Grant asked Thomas who had ordered the men to keep going, but nobody had; it had been a decision of the moment on the part of the men making the charge. Supposedly Grant mumbled, "Someone will suffer for it, if it turns out badly." Of course, it did not turn out badly. Grant later claimed to have given Thomas authority to take the ridge, but the facts indicate otherwise. No doubt, Grant's ego did not allow him to admit in writing that one of the great charges of the war was a soldiers' charge, not one he ordered. The collapse of Bragg's center meant the collapse of his whole line, and only a determined rearguard defense by Cleburne prevented an even more serious Confederate disaster. Bragg retreated south; eventually Joseph Johnston replaced him, and Bragg wound up as a military adviser to Jefferson Davis in Richmond.[23]

Grant, delighted with his success, wired news of the victory to Washington, prepared supplies for Burnside, and ordered two corps to his relief. Longstreet, getting wind of Grant's attempts to trap him, gave up his flawed efforts to besiege Knoxville and retreated to Greenville, Tennessee; eventually, he crossed back into Virginia to rejoin the Army of Northern Virginia. Burnside let him go and was later relieved of his command (though he too wound up back in Virginia), for his decision not to pursue meant that Grant had to leave a contingent of troops in East Tennessee to protect against any possible renewed operations by Longstreet—which never happened.

Grant later commented, "The victory at Chattanooga was won against greater odds, considering the advantage the enemy had of position, and was accomplished more easily than was expected by reason of Bragg's making several grave mistakes: first, in sending away his ablest corps commander with over twenty thousand troops; second, in sending away a division of troops on the eve of battle; third, in placing so much of a force on the plain in front of his impregnable position." Grant understood that he had been fortunate. Here, as early in the war and during the latter stages of the Vicksburg campaign, a lack of skilled Confederate leadership had done much to assist him in gaining his objectives. Still, for such opportunities to mean anything, they had to be taken advantage of, and Grant had done that, mostly by a sensible and uncomplicated approach to strategy and tactics. His challenge at Chattanooga had not been complicated; what he had to do was clear to him, and he deserved credit for getting it done—unlike many other Union generals.[24]

Grant also made sure that Sherman received much credit for the victory, yet in truth Sherman's performance had been below par; he had moved slowly, doing little to carry out his part of the overall plan. Pat Cleburne withdrew because of Thomas's success in the center, not because of Sherman's pressure. Grant did not, however, praise Thomas. His friendship with Sherman was too deep for Grant to say anything negative about his trusted subordinate, and a win was a win. Sherman had always been there for him, and Grant never forgot—just as he never forgot that Thomas had hesitated to obey orders.[25]

Aside from the obvious military success, which resulted in the Confederates losing a vital rail center and giving the Union an opportunity to invade Georgia, Grant had something else to be proud of. In his memoirs he noted the cooperation of units from three distinct armies that had never fought together before: the Army of the Tennessee, which Grant knew and understood and was commanded by his confidant, Sherman; the Army of the Cumberland, commanded by Thomas; and elements of the Army of the Potomac, led by Hooker. They had managed to coordinate their efforts and produce a decisive victory. Grant commented, "There was no jealousy—hardly rivalry," which may or may not have been true, but if there was any, it did not interfere with achieving victory. Aside from Thomas's occasional recalcitrance, Grant had put together a team very quickly, mainly by counting heavily on Sherman and Vicksburg campaign troops, and his determination to do what had to be done seemed contagious. That he came to Chattanooga riding a wave of success may have made Thomas and Hooker more inclined to cooperate with him. He had already gained the admiration and gratitude of Thomas's army by opening the cracker line, and he had involved each army in the campaign in a way that made its role significant.[26]

The confidence that Grant showed when he led his army inland below Vicksburg had grown and matured. He had encountered obstacles at Chattanooga and suffered some sleepless nights but did not let his worries get him down. As in the past, he kept pushing ahead, making changes as needed, reassuring his government, and sticking to the task until it was done. This was the Grant that two years in the western theater of war had produced, the Grant that would now be asked by Lincoln to turn the tide of war in the eastern theater.

NOTES

1. Grant, *Memoirs*, 390–91; *OR*, ser. 1, vol. 31, pt. 2, pp. 22–24, 569.

2. Grant, *Memoirs*, 403; Simon, *Papers of Grant*, 9:281, 296; Simpson, *Grant*, 226.

3. Simon, *Papers of Grant*, 9:298; Grant, *Memoirs*, 403–4.

4. Simon, *Papers of Grant*, 9:299; Grant, *Memoirs*, 404–9.

5. Simon, *Papers of Grant*, 9:296–97, 302.

6. Grant, *Memoirs*, 409–10; Simpson, *Grant*, 227.

7. Grant, *Memoirs*, 410; Simon, *Papers of Grant*, 304, 305, 308.

8. Grant, *Memoirs*, 410–11; Simon, *Papers of Grant*, 9:317, 320.

9. Grant, *Memoirs*, 411–12; Simpson, *Grant*, 141, 228–29; *OR*, ser. 1, vol. 17, pt. 2, p. 3; Peter Cozzens, *The Shipwreck of Their Hopes: The Battles for Chattanooga* (Urbana, IL, 1994), 45–46.

10. Grant, *Memoirs*, 413; Simon, *Papers of Grant*, 9:321; Simpson, *Grant*, 229.

11. Grant, *Memoirs*, 413–14; Simpson, *Grant*, 229–30.

12. Grant, *Memoirs*, 414, 417–18; Simpson, *Grant*, 231; Cozzens, *Shipwreck*, 18, 20, 47, 69–73.

13. James Lee McDonough, *Chattanooga: A Death Grip on the Confederacy* (Knoxville, TN, 1984), 98, 100; Grant, *Memoirs*, 424–25.

14. Grant, *Memoirs*, 422–23; Simon, *Papers of Grant*, 9:311–12.

15. Grant, *Memoirs*, 425–26; Simon, *Papers of Grant*, 9:393. Grant's report on Chattanooga operations is in *OR*, ser. 1, vol. 31, pt. 2, pp. 27–37.

16 .Grant, *Memoirs*, 424–30; Simon, *Papers of Grant*, 9:411–12.

17. Grant, *Memoirs*, 431.

18. Ibid., 433–35; Cozzens, *Shipwreck*, 126–35.

19. Grant, *Memoirs*, 434, 436, 443; Cozzens, *Shipwreck*, 146–58 passim; *OR*, ser. 1, vol. 31, pt. 2, p. 32.

20. Grant, *Memoirs*, 439–41; Cozzens, *Shipwreck*, 159–78; *OR*, ser. 1, vol. 31, pt. 2, p. 678.

21. Grant, *Memoirs*, 441; *OR*, ser. 1, vol. 32, pt. 2, pp. 25, 27.

22. Grant, *Memoirs*, 441; Cozzens, *Shipwreck*, 204–43.

23. Grant, *Memoirs*, 445–47; Joseph S. Fullerton, "The Army of the Cumberland at Chattanooga," in Johnson and Buell, *Battles and Leaders of the Civil War*, 3:725; Cozzens, *Shipwreck*, 247–332 passim, 391; *OR*, ser. 1, vol. 32, pt. 2, pp. 34–35.

24. Grant, *Memoirs*, 448–49, 458; Simon, *Papers of Grant*, 9:446, 454, 458.

25. Cozzens, *Shipwreck*, 391–92.

26. Grant, *Memoirs*, 448.

Chapter Twelve

Wrapping Up Service in the West

With Chattanooga and Knoxville secure, Grant established his winter headquarters in Nashville, which seemed a central location for administrative duties. He was expecting to retain his command and personally lead a campaign to capture Atlanta. He also held to his desire to march on Mobile, or perhaps Savannah, once Atlanta had been taken. Meanwhile, he toured East Tennessee to check on possible supply routes for future operations, and probably to get away from his headquarters and paperwork. He returned to Nashville in mid-January 1864.

During this period, he had a peculiar confrontation with Secretary of War Stanton, who had the authority to control telegraph operations, for security reasons, and he was not timid in exercising it. Grant, however, wanted his own man running the Nashville telegraph, someone he knew and trusted. He managed, by threatening punishment, to get the government operator to give up the key; the telegrapher apparently feared Grant more than Stanton. This incident happened before Grant left for his East Tennessee trip, and when he returned, he found "quite a commotion": the War Department had "reprimanded" the operator "very severely" and fired him for giving up the telegraph. Grant immediately sent word to Washington that the man could not be relieved for merely obeying orders and later recalled, probably with some glee, also saying that "it was absolutely necessary for me to have the cipher, and the man would most certainly have been punished if he had not delivered it; that they would have to punish me if they punished anybody, or words to that effect." That settled that, and the Grant who stood up for himself presented quite a contrast to the woeful general who had considered resigning after Shiloh. He had been a victim once of Stanton's loose system, which had permitted a disloyal telegrapher to wreak havoc with military correspondence during the Forts Henry and Donelson campaign. Grant intended that it should not happen again.[1]

Next, looking to departmental deployment, he told Sherman to spread his forces along the railroad from Chattanooga to Nashville. Sherman objected, preferring instead to go back to Mississippi and clear out any inland threats to Vicksburg. Confederate forces still roamed though eastern Mississippi, and though they were too small to have any hope of retaking Vicksburg, their mere presence caused concern about that city's security. Grant assented; Sherman returned to Vicksburg and marched his army across the center of the state, driving meek resistance before him and further destroying Rebel supplies and the railroad junction at Meridian. A part of his effort failed when Bedford Forrest drove Sooy Smith's cavalry back to Memphis, but otherwise Sherman's Meridian campaign was a success.[2]

Grant did not blame Sherman for Forrest's success; in fact, he had a high opinion of the man whom Sherman termed a "devil." In his memoirs, applauding "the particular kind of warfare which Forrest had carried on," Grant asserted that "neither army could present a more effective officer than he was." As a general who had come to understand and value officers who made good use of their abilities, Grant appreciated the military record of one of the South's most controversial generals. Of course, those laudatory comments came long after the war, when old soldiers tended to be generous with one another.[3]

Grant ordered George Thomas to pressure Joseph Johnston's army in northern Georgia, and he also sent reinforcements to East Tennessee to John Foster, who had replaced Burnside, and later to John Schofield, who replaced Foster. As things turned out, Schofield did not need any help to fight Longstreet, who had given up operating in Tennessee. Grant again found Thomas reluctant to move and had to issue more than one order. Shortly after Thomas advanced, however, he pulled back to Chattanooga, insisting that logistical problems were too great to risk an offensive. Grant, who had been concerned about the health of his son and worried enough to take a quick trip to St. Louis, had also to deal with a chronically slow general with whom he had had tense relations ever since arriving in Chattanooga. Then, on March 3, 1864, Grant learned that he would soon have more than one general, or even a few armies, to worry about.[4]

On March 9, Grant was promoted to lieutenant general (a rank that had been restored a few days earlier by an act of Congress) and called to Washington to consult with Abraham Lincoln personally. Halleck requested that Lincoln give Halleck's position of commanding general of all Union armies to Grant; Halleck stayed on as his chief of staff. Grant now had control of the Federal grand strategy to prosecute the war. Ultimately, he gave Sherman his command in the West while he himself traveled with the Army of the Potomac in the East, which continued to be under the direct command of George Meade.

Reflecting in his memoirs upon his decision to move to the eastern theater, he wrote: "It had been my intention . . . to remain in the West, even if I was made lieutenant-general; but when I got to Washington and saw the situation it was plain that here was the point for the commanding general to be. No one else could, probably, resist the pressure that would be brought to bear upon him to desist from his own plans and pursue others." His words underscored his transition from Grant the uncertain and sometimes timid warrior to Grant the confident commander.[5]

The building blocks that had transformed Grant from a cadet who did not want a military career into Lincoln's best general were many. His natural determination and grit made a firm foundation for later experiences, in and out of the military. At West Point he had developed his powers of observing others, which would help him in the future but also occasionally failed him. In Mexico he saw that maneuver cost less than frontal assaults, and he passed the test of courage in standing up to the terrors and rigors of battle. He learned further that style, including dress, was not a measure of ability. Grant no doubt delighted in finding that a good general could be himself, without the "fuss and feathers" of a Winfield Scott, and still earn the respect and affection of the men he led—the men who made it possible for a general to rise or fall. Under Scott, however, Grant had the opportunity to study extreme logistical problems and their solutions. Here he observed that an army could cut itself loose from its base and still succeed although, in fact, an army that left its base behind could still draw supplies from it, thanks to wagons and escorts. Grant's later assertion that he cut himself loose from his base did not make that distinction.

In his personal life between wars, Grant faced challenges that would have overwhelmed a less resolute human being. The friction between his and his wife's families over the slavery issue kept up an undercurrent of uncertainty as he juggled the possibilities of obtaining financial help from relatives. His inability to be a tough-minded businessman kept him from progressing in the mercantile world, and the resulting blows to his pride must have kept him awake through many miserable nights. Finally, he had had to depend upon his father and brothers to support his family, as he continued to be burdened by debts and depressed by the inability to find a suitable niche. Only his strong will, underscoring the innate strength of his personality, kept him going, and in a sense his various business failures helped prepare him for the military politics and bloody battlefields to come. Grant never turned his back on his responsibilities, never tried to bail out, and never tried to blame others for his misfortunes—qualities that may have not helped him in the nonmilitary world but enhanced his generalship.

Although Grant found politics in general and political machinations in particular quite distasteful, he learned from his earliest days in the Civil War that they were realities; he could either ignore them or use them to his advantage. At times he had trouble distinguishing what was best for him to do—whether to keep quiet, to prod gently, or to protest loudly. Over time, however, he learned the nuances of politics, and the more confident he became as a general, the more confidence he had in his ability to get politicians to see things his way.

Grant's growth as a commander in campaigns and battles took longer to develop, though there were common themes throughout the first two years of the war. Although his tenacity and resolve were his anchors throughout, he made mistakes. For a time he tended to underestimate his enemies, which almost cost him Belmont, Fort Donelson, and Shiloh. Yet those experiences brought another of his qualities to the fore: his ability to adjust to situations and keep on going. Grant had amazing resiliency, and even in desperate battlefield situations he refused to cower. In his darkest days, while he was, in effect, shelved in the wake of Shiloh, Grant had his most tenacious struggle with himself. His pride had not been so battered since his business failure days, and his depression reached a point that resignation, or at least reassignment, seemed inescapable. Yet he stayed the course, though the impact on his psyche would be evident for months afterward.

Once returned to command, Grant made flawed battle plans for the attack on Iuka and seemed uncharacteristically uninterested in the campaign and battle. Worse, he shifted all blame from himself to a subordinate and followed up by refusing to allow that same subordinate to pursue a badly battered Confederate army after the fight at Corinth. This Sam Grant was a shadow of what he had been and would become afterward, making the period between the battles of Iuka and Corinth and the northern Mississippi campaign his most crucial of the war. He could have gone either way as a commander: he could have bounced back, or he could have descended further into uncertainty, timidity, and disingenuousness. The worry that still haunted him after the beginning of the siege of Vicksburg, when he continually fretted about Johnston, showed the depth of the post-Shiloh scars.

Fortunately for the Union cause, he kept going, though at times it was no more than a steady plodding, putting one foot in front of the other. The setbacks at Holly Springs and Chickasaw Bayou taught him lessons about careless logistics and hurried preparations. He seemed to learn, too, that allowing personal feelings, such as his disgust with McClernand, to creep into his military planning could produce disastrous results: extending his supply line too far, for instance, and sending Sherman downriver, both in an attempt to finish the job on the Mississippi before a political hack like McClernand arrived. He never liked John McClernand, but he chose to make good use of him as long as he needed him, rather than risk the success of operations to keep him at arm's length. Moreover, Grant discovered that subtlety produced much better results when he wanted something from Washington than did loud complaining and badgering.

The Vicksburg campaign ultimately proved to be Grant's finest hour, though he struggled and endured many disappointments. His experiences reinforced a lesson that had slowly come to him earlier in the war: the need for a team of subordinates upon whom he could depend, people he could trust to take care of business. So he learned to endure McClernand. It did not matter that Sherman, McPherson, and Porter did not like the man either, just as long as McClernand did his job and the others did not let their feelings keep them from doing theirs. Grant's desire to be surrounded by generals he could count on was apparent when he moved on to Chattanooga, taking Sherman with him as well as a division from McPherson, another trusted lieutenant. It was not easy for him to mold a new team when he moved east and traveled with the Army of the Potomac, but he had by then come to understand clearly that fighting a war successfully depended upon teamwork above all else.

The Vicksburg campaign demonstrated the crux of Grant's strategic and tactical philosophies. Having learned the negatives of frontal assaults in Mexico, though he occasionally used such attacks, he avoided them whenever possible. At Belmont he tried an indirect approach, along with the cooperation of the navy, and when he did order a frontal charge to try to win the battle, he left his own flank vulnerable and no doubt wished he had practiced what he preached. He also ordered a head-on attack at Donelson, but he got away with it there, thanks to inept Confederate leadership and the demoralization of enemy troops. At Shiloh he relied on superior numbers in launching the counterattack that helped recover lost ground and turn the tide.

Much more Grant-like was the Iuka campaign, in which he maneuvered to catch Sterling Price between two wings of his army, and he also used flank movements in northern Mississippi. Diversions became his trademark, and he had refined diversionary tactics to a fine art by the time his army crossed the Mississippi below Vicksburg. One of Grant's strengths was to recognize advantages that he had created, even if they came about unintentionally. Indeed, diversions helped decide the course of Vicksburg operations in the Union's favor, and Grant continued to depend on deception and flanking attacks at Chattanooga.

The key to understanding how Grant's mind worked, as others have observed, lies in his commonsense approach. He admired those who had academic knowledge of military science, such as Sherman and Halleck, and knew he did not measure up as a student of the military arts; as he admitted, he had not spent much time at West Point reading about strategy and tactics. Nevertheless, he could look at maps, examine enemy positions, and come up with plans simple in design but devastating to the enemy if properly executed. One thing he learned quickly was that by keeping his own army busy, he could keep the enemy off balance. Even when his operations failed, he maintained the initiative by making opponents uncertain of his next moves. That his envelopment and deception concepts were not complex made it easier for subordinates to use citizen-soldier troops to carry them out. (Perhaps his simple, straightforward approach to military science gives a hint of his admiration for Bedford Forrest, who operated in much the same manner and with considerable success.)[6]

Despite occasional disaffection, Grant's soldiers appreciated a leader who never could be satisfied doing nothing. Grant recognized that by keeping his army active, he kept their hopes alive for victory and an end to the war so they could go home. With his shabby attire and demeanor, Grant never inspired awe among his

U. S. Grant, ca. 1865. From Ezra J. Warner, *Generals in Blue: Lives of the Union Commanders* (Baton Rouge: Louisiana State University Press, 1964), 184.

troops, but his stubborn refusal to quit, to keep on trying no matter the circumstances, deeply impressed the hard-nosed, midwestern character of so many of his men. He understood that connection and drew strength from it—perhaps even cultivated it, just by being himself. He was never flashy, but his dedication to duty was a quality that played well in the ranks.

Grant's ability to understand basic concepts helped him grasp another truism that he used to great advantage. Campaigning in the western theater required dealing effectively with rivers, which could be a help or a nuisance, depending upon circumstances. Grant realized early on that if he developed a good reputation with the Union navy or, more particularly, naval commanders, the rivers could be a plus in his operations. Beginning with Belmont, then, and continuing through the surrender of Vicksburg, Grant and the navy became a formidable two-pronged force in the West. His close relationship with David Porter proved especially rewarding, both personally and to the Union cause.

Those who disparage Grant's military career have always been quick to point out that despite his obvious qualities as a general, he made his pre-eastern theater reputation against second- and third-rate Confederate generals. It must be pointed out, though, that no other Union general did as well against that same cast of characters. It is one thing to have opportunities presented by enemy generals who possess at best limited abilities; it is quite another to take full advantage of them. History's best commanders grasp those moments and use them well, no matter who their opponents may be. It must also be recognized that Grant, especially during the Vicksburg campaign, did not sit around waiting for enemy commanders to make mistakes. An active general, he learned quickly that by pushing his forces in various directions, he created problems for his adversaries, which in turn created openings for him. Grant's plaudits for Vicksburg were well earned, for the successful outcome of the campaign was not handed to him on a platter; he was its architect, and the fact that John Pemberton made it easier says more about Grant's talents than Pemberton's shortcomings.

Grant is often compared with Robert E. Lee, especially during never-ending debates over who was the better general. Both had benefited from inferior competition before they faced each other in Virginia in 1864. Lee had the advantage of fighting on home ground, among friendly supporters, on the relatively narrow strip of land that made up the Virginia theater. He rarely had to deal with badgering politicians or subordinates jealous of his success. He got into trouble twice when he invaded unfriendly territory, resulting in defeat at Antietam and Gettysburg. Grant had had a much bigger expanse of territory to conquer, most of it dominated by unfriendly civilians. He experienced major problems when dealing with jealous fellow generals and anxious politicians. His whole Civil War experience was spent in invading enemy territory and confronting all the problems, especially of a logistical nature, that such invasions entail, though it was also true that he had considerably more resources from which to draw. Clearly, however, through the end of 1863, Grant had faced more disadvantages than Lee.

The Grant who came to Virginia in 1864 had traveled a long, rocky road and survived. Descriptive adjectives such as strong-willed, tenacious, flexible, commonsensical, politically skilled, logistically astute, team-oriented, and determined all fit him well. All that he had become had been bred into him through a process of lessons learned on and off the battlefield. His rise to general in chief of all the Union armies gave him a position long awaiting an appropriate leader; after enduring lesser men in the job, Abraham Lincoln had finally found the right fit. Ulysses Grant had turned the course of war decisively in the West, and now he had been asked to do the same in the East. He lived up to those expectations.

NOTES

1. Grant, *Memoirs*, 458–71; Grant, *Papers of Grant*, 10:14–16, 48–49, 79–82.

2. Simon, *Papers of Grant*, 10:19–24; Grant, *Memoirs*, 463–65. On Meridian, see Margie Riddle Bearss, *Sherman's Forgotten Campaign: The Meridian Expedition* (Baltimore, MD, 1987). See also Jack Hurst, *Nathan Bedford Forrest: A Biography* (New York, 1993), 149–55; *OR*, ser. 1, vol. 39, pt. 2, p. 121.

3. Grant, *Memoirs*, 464.

4. Ibid., 466; Simon, *Papers of Grant*, 10:64–65, 86, 98, 102, 109, 115–17, 119, 151, 163, 174.

5. Simon, *Papers of Grant*, 10:186–89, 195; Grant, *Memoirs*, 469–71.

6. For examples of Grant's comments on Sherman and Halleck, see Grant, *Memoirs*, 364–65; and Simon, *Papers of Grant*, 5:225–26.

BIBLIOGRAPHICAL NOTE

Grant's military career can be tracked through a variety of sources. The most significant primary sources include Grant's own memoirs, originally published in two volumes. The edition I prefer is Ulysses S. Grant, *Personal Memoirs of U. S. Grant: Selected Letters, 1839–1865* (New York, 1990), which combines both volumes into one and thus facilitates their use. Readers should be aware, however, that page numbers in this cited edition do not correspond to those of the original two published volumes.

The War of the Rebellion: A Compilation of the Official Records of the Union and Confederate Armies, 128 vols. (Washington, DC, 1880–1891), is absolutely essential to an understanding of Grant's role in the war. Also helpful is the 35-volume set titled *Official Records of the Union and Confederate Navies in the War of the Rebellion* (Washington, DC, 1894–1927). Since Grant orchestrated several joint operations in the western theater, many items pertaining to his activities appear in the naval records.

John Y. Simon, ed., *The Papers of U. S. Grant*, 22 volumes to date (Carbondale, IL, 1967–ㅤ), is another compilation of primary documents necessary for any study of Grant. Thoroughly researched and extensively annotated, it is a wonderful and remarkably easy-to-use resource.

Three noteworthy modern biographies of Grant are William S. McFeely, *Grant: A Biography* (New York, 1981); Brooks D. Simpson, *Ulysses S. Grant: Triumph over Adversity, 1822–1865* (Boston, MA, 2000), the first of two projected volumes; and Jean Edward Smith, *Grant* (New York, 2001).

Many useful collateral works include several excellent biographies of generals and others who were in a position to know Grant well; battle and campaign studies of the Civil War in the western theater through 1863 and in the eastern theater in 1864–65 also contain much information on Grant's military career. Many of these are cited in the chapter notes in this volume.

INDEX

Sherman, William T. (*continued*)
101–104, 110; and Grant, 26, 39,
44, 53, 54, 59, 60, 62, 78, 82, 84,
133, 134, 166; during land
campaign, assaults and siege of
Vicksburg operations, 121, 123–
28, 130–32, 135–41, 145, 147;
during North Mississippi
operations, 68, 86–89; at Shiloh,
48, 51, 55
Shiloh, Campaign and Battle of,
47–56
Simpson, Brooks, 26
Slavery, 7, 8, 96
Smith, Charles Ferguson, 15, 17–
18, 25–26, 29, 32, 35, 36, 38–39,
41, 48
Smith, W. F., 155–57
Stanton, Edwin, 42, 82, 89, 92, 98,
99, 106, 141, 151, 152, 161, 169
Steele, Frederick, Greenville
expedition of, 112
Steele's Bayou and Deer Creek
Campaign, 102–104
Stevenson, Carter, 129–31, 162
Stuart, David, 51

Tennessee River, 27, 30, 31, 32
Thayer, John, 35, 36
Thomas, George, 29, 59, 152–56,
159–61, 164–67, 170
Thompson, Jeff, 14, 17, 18, 25–26
Tilghman, Lloyd, 34

United States Military Academy.
See West Point

Van Dorn, Earl, 48, 54, 67,
68, 69, 70, 75, 76, 77, 78,
81; raid on Holly Springs,
90–91
Vicksburg Campaign: assaults
and siege of Vicksburg, 135–
47; surrender of Vicksburg,
145–47; Grant's attempts to
bypass, 95–106, 109–15 (*see
also* Grant–Williams Canal;
Lake Providence project;
Yazoo Pass Campaign; Steele's
Bayou and Deer Creek Cam-
paign; Duckport project; Grand
Gulf, Battle of); inland campaign, 119–32 (*see also* Port
Gibson, Battle of; Raymond,
Battle of; Jackson, Battle of;
Champion Hill, Battle of; Big
Black, Battle of); in North
Mississippi, 81–91

Walke, Henry, 20, 22, 26
Walker, John, 144
Wallace, Lew, 35, 36, 38, 48, 50, 51,
54, 56
Wallace, W. H. L., 17, 18, 48, 50, 51,
54
Washburne, Elihu, 12, 42, 43, 59,
66, 120
West Point, 1–3
Wilson, James, 143

Yates, Richard, 11, 120
Yazoo Pass Campaign, 97, 101–102,
104, 109